La Moneda after September 11, 1973

CHILE
from within

President Salvador Allende and first lady Hortensia Bussi
on the balcony of the presidential palace La Moneda, 1970

Proclamation No. 7
(Warning)

The Junta of the Military Government hereby
advises the population:

1. All persons resisting the new Government
should be aware of the consequences.

2. All industries, housing units, and businesses
shall cease resistance immediately or the Armed
Forces shall proceed with the same energy and
decision evident in its attack on La Moneda, the
Presidential Palace.

3. The Junta of the Military Government hereby
announces that, while having no intention to
destroy, if public order is in any way disrupted by
disobedience to its decrees, it will not hesitate to
act with the same energy and decision which the
citizenry has already had occasion to observe.

Signed: Governing Junta of the Armed Forces
and Police of Chile.

Santiago, September 11, 1973

La Moneda open to the public

CHILE
from within
1 9 7 3   1 9 8 8

P H O T O G R A P H S   B Y

PAZ ERRAZURIZ • ALEJANDRO HOPPE • ALVARO HOPPE

HELEN HUGHES • JORGE IANISZEWSKI • HECTOR LOPEZ

KENA LORENZINI • J. D. MARINELLO • CHRISTIAN MONTECINO

MARCELO MONTECINO • OSCAR NAVARRO • CLAUDIO PEREZ

LUIS POIROT • PAULO SLACHEVSKY • LUIS WEINSTEIN

OSCAR WITTKE

T E X T S   B Y
MARCO ANTONIO DE LA PARRA
ARIEL DORFMAN

E D I T E D
W I T H
SUSAN MEISELAS

W.W. NORTON & COMPANY   NEW YORK LONDON

Printed and bound by *Dai Nippon Printing Co., Ltd.*, Tokyo, Japan.

The text of this book is composed in Helvetica.
Composition by Trufont Typographers, Inc.
Book design by Sergio Pérez Ramirez.

First Edition.

ISBN 0-393-02817-8
ISBN 0-393-30653-4 pbk

W. W. Norton & Company, Inc., 500 Fifth Avenue, New York, N.Y. 10110

W.W. Norton & Company, Ltd., 37 Great Russell Street, London WC1B 3NU

1 2 3 4 5 6 7 8 9 0

CONTENTS

ACKNOWLEDGMENTS

This book could not have been made without the support of many people. Helen Hughes and Juan O'Brien shared their home, Sergio Perez his patience; Jay Nubile printed endless days and La Escuela de Estudios Superiores donated its darkroom. There is special thanks to Marcelo Montealegre and Alma Guillermoprieto for their generous time and Cynthia Brown for her encouragement. We are grateful to the Arca Foundation and the Fund for Free Expression, and especially to Jaime Barrios.

FRAGMENTS OF A SELF-PORTRAIT

MARCO ANTONIO DE LA PARRA

TRANSLATED BY MARCELO MONTEALEGRE

In a sense, these are photos from our most secret family album. Here we find our relatives who are cops, two uncles who are in the military, the cousin who was a bodyguard for high authorities of the regime, another who is a commando, a third who operated certain units of police intelligence in the provinces, a fourth who wrote to us from his exile in Germany, or Sweden, or Mozambique. Also there, implicitly, is the nephew who died, gunned down trying to prevent the kidnapping of two fellow teachers, who would be discovered two days later, their throats slashed, in the fields of Quilicura. Here are the aunts who gave their jewels for the national reconstruction after the promises of the coup, the aunts who banged their empty pots in opposition to Allende, the aunts who did it against Pinochet, and the aunts who did it on both occasions. The younger brother who quickly took down the leftist posters from his walls to toss them on the fire where they burned all forbidden sympathies. And all those girlfriends wooed and won over with endless phone calls on long drawn-out curfew nights when others, myself included, all of us, even made parties under the metallic laughter of the helicopters and the phantasmagoric apparition of a searchlight that protected our dreams, free of evil or dangerous happenings. All those I recall from some distant childhood when we gathered under the family trellises for a barbecue, shared amid the general laughter and joking before settling down to play bingo, at which I never once won a prize.

Here are the coffins, the luxury sport cars, the department stores, the credit cards, the soccer headlines, the weddings held in daylight so that the midnight police patrol would not interrupt the reception. Implicit in these photos are the barricades of burning tires, the books slipped by contraband, the photos we did not take: going to work as if nothing, or crying out in a stadium filled with ghosts, visiting a friend held prisoner in an abandoned beach resort, the photos we refused to look at, those we found intolerable to remember.

That daily calm, fragile, volatile, just barely sustained, the calm not photographed, was exactly what urged these photos to be taken.

These photos are our ghosts and our shadows, our mangled guardian angels ringing in our ear that we Chileans are a family. They serve us as memory, evocation, nostalgia; they are indispensable. To know who we are, and who we were while we could not recognize our own reflections, stunned by the familiarity of the daily bursts of machinegun fire interrupting the TV serial that came after the news, the trivial sting of tear gas in our eyes as we chose a pair of shoes in the shadow of a traffic light.

Meanwhile, kids grow up, go to school, graduate, learn to talk, sometimes ask me to tell them about democracy. And we try not to take our wounds too seriously, to shrug, to understate things the way Chileans do.

For fifteen years the government insisted that the

country was in full color. As we can see in these photos, we were dreaming in gray, the color of gunpowder.

The first (and oldest) photograph in the book shows Salvador Allende and his wife on a balcony in La Moneda, the presidential palace, waving handkerchiefs to a virtual multitude, where the photographer has submerged himself so that we might be the silent beneficiaries of that trivial gesture, maybe done enthusiastically in front of an exhilarated crowd; but, in the light of events, with that tragic force that photography always reveals (its revenge against the superficiality with which it is used), it rather seems that Allende and his wife are saying goodbye. We will not see them again in the book. The photograph proves painful beyond any ideology.

The same bombed out balcony on the next page is a necessary redundancy. All the impact is already present in the first one, in the tilt of Allende's head, in a certain immodest innocence of Hortensia Bussi, his wife, in the suicidal naiveté of the handkerchiefs.

The third image is a wide-angle view of La Moneda, days after the bombings, when everyone, heathens and Christians alike, came in bewilderment to contemplate the wounds of the war many believed ended. The visible evidence of power, what we never imagined our eyes would behold, wondering if our nightmares, yearnings, and/or fear could be real.

This book continues with that task, that observation, that visit. From these visible mutilations they made these plates, the invisible leave their trace in the margins, the serendipity, the poetic act of each frame (a job for historians, novelists, dramatists to give a name to things).

This book is also a kind of exorcism. These images take with them the souls of the dead. They conjure up the assassins, cast out our worse demons. We need to look at them again and again. They are part of the history of how Chile was changed forever, the history of a mutation, of a metamorphosis. In the last images, the wounds of the missiles tossed at La Moneda by the Hawker-Hunters have healed, but the scars remain, indelible. To laugh again, freely and irresponsibly, will be an act with political meaning. To dream again would be an entire revolution.

The omnipresent television screen with the faces of the top members of the Pinochet regime has not been in vain. We have all become addicted to consumption; we are all specialists in panic, experts in Japanese radios, like the peasant from Chiloé you might see praying devoutly in front of a shop window crammed with imported goods. We were all General Pinochet, or General Sinclair, decorated like a Renaissance cardinal; we all bear on our backs the open wounds on which we can read the weekend sports headlines. I too bombed La Moneda, I too was taken to the National Stadium, I denied the torture on a TV musical show, I asked in desperation where I was, and nobody, not even I, could give an answer.

These photos are a struggle for lucidity, an effort to separate image from sentiment, ideas from facts. They were taken against risks made custom, sometimes with confiscated cameras, broken, at times hidden, others surreptitiously from within a crowd, urgently. They were taken with blind faith, in a moment of mystical ecstasy, the craft of martyrs (who wasn't a martyr in those times?). The dedication of this book shows this has not changed.

Here are images that give us back our eyes. That turn us in and redeem us. We were irresolute, oblique; we hid our hands, lowered our eyes. Those who spoke up, stood up straight, were the few. But at the same time these photographs show the country did not submit, we kept life vibrant, our hearts alive.

These scenes allow us to know the extent of our pain. They offer images that will give rise to words and thus will salvage the mental powers of a country where they tried to make us believe that politics was the devil's language and that God was a microphone. But we already know that heaven does not wear a uniform, and that angels do not shoot from unmarked cars. The country neither began nor ended on September 11, 1973. The mythology concludes. History begins again. We can think anew.

It is not superfluous to remember that in one of the many gyrations of censorship (I do not remember the date; one head cannot hold that many bad memories) opposition magazines were forbidden to print photographs. Their writers, in a surrealistic move of the sort that has made Kafka more or less our foremost teller of tales and Alfred Jarry the most apt singer of our reality, left white spaces with captions underneath, maintaining headlines and describing in the empty space what the photo represented. This was not happenstance, or Zen-like foolishness, but the perfect metaphor for what we saw around us. Blind by decree, we heard of things that our cruel and terrorized imaginations distorted to exhaustion. We came to fear our own shadows, as if all the mirrors had been placed under arrest.

This book is a sort of revenge by the censored, the release of stifled imagination, almost dazed from looking itself in the eye.

Unlike many books of photographs that arise out of journalistic interest in a nation torn by conflict (violence is always irresistibly exotic), this volume has been created entirely from within, by witnesses who lived what they focused on, in some ways like frag-

ments of a self-portrait, avoiding any contact with curiosity, mere information, or aesthetic contemplation of any kind. These photos were taken on the run, riding the waves of the suffering of those years, a sort of defense against the atmosphere of war that floated for a time, always so much longer than one would have wanted. These photos are an exercise in liberty, an effort to survive, a decision to go on living rather than perpetuate the impotence and guilt of being a passive spectator. Capturing the image was the only way not to become a victim of the reality, a pawn of events, to participate in some small way in the history of our country.

These images had to be taken by people who *lived* in Chile, from within, developed within the deafening din of an unending time, through the very same habits the function of photography was trying to break. These images are confessional, suicidal; it hurt to take them. I will confront the pain, says the artist, I will dream what my people, what I myself do not dare to dream. In spite of themselves, these photographers took pictures, sometimes not knowing of what. Later, in the darkroom, in the exhibition gallery, with the passage of time, they discovered what they had made. The photos will never stop developing.

Everything that ought to be written about my country has not yet been written, nor has it been possible even to think what needs to be thought. Only recently have the elements aligned themselves into a semblance of peace, and this book, I assume and hope, is a sign of this. It appears at a time when (we hope) it will not be necessary to use it as denunciation, or as a contribution to some legendary struggle. It waits for the curtain to fall on these years.

And it waits, hoping.

Commander-in-Chief of the Armed Forces Augusto Pinochet Ugarte addresses the nation

Shortly before curfew, Santiago

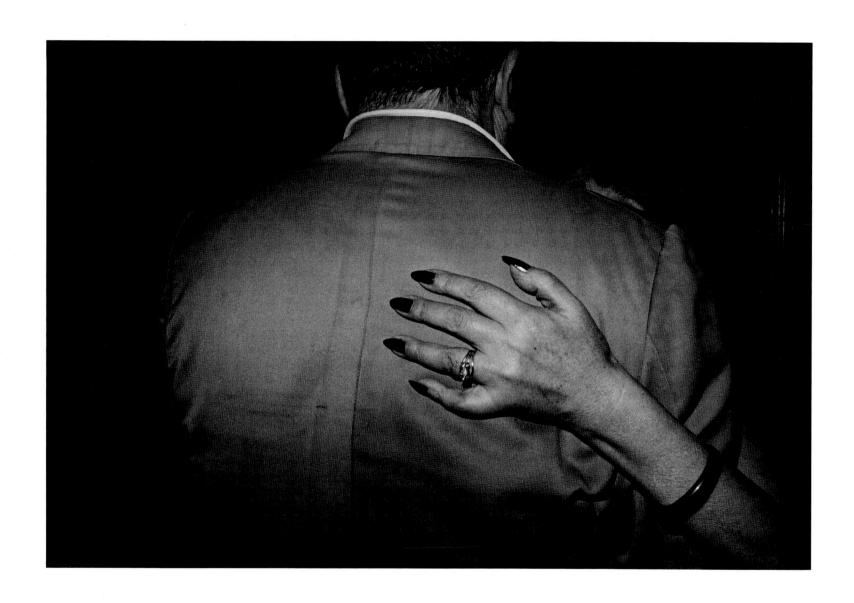

6   Bar, Santiago

Chonchi, island of Chiloe

Santiago

Detention, Santiago

10

La Victoria barrio, Santiago

11

Valdivia, southern Chile

La Dehesa, Santiago

Commemoration of poet Pablo
Neruda, Santiago

13

Senior citizens club, San Bernardo

14

15

Pirque, suburb of Santiago

Curanilahue, southern Chile

17

Paposo, northern Chile

Celebration of the Virgin of the Rosary, Andacollo

Communal meal, Villa Francia, Santiago

Land takeover "Raul Silva
Henriquez," outskirts of
Santiago

20

Mapuche Indians, Puerto Dominquez

Santiago

Santiago

Santiago

General Sinclair at high mass, Santiago

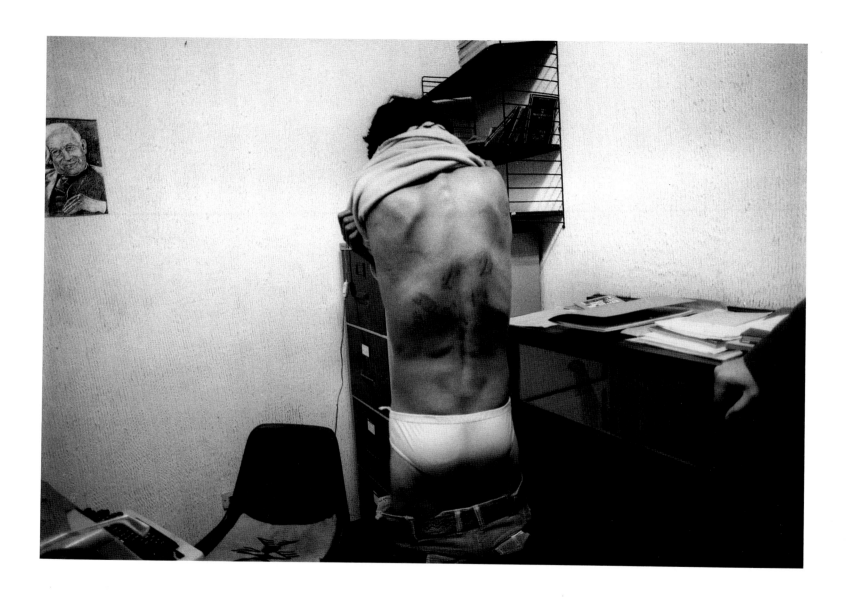

Inside the Vicaria, human rights office

Specially appointed judge-prosecutor

Wake for Jose Manuel Parada, human rights worker kidnapped and assassinated

Funeral for Felipe Antonio, aged four, killed by military in Peñalolen

Vigil for the detained and disappeared

31

Land takeover, Puente Alto

Weekly vigil by the families of the victims of repression in front of La Moneda 32

33

Detention, downtown Santiago

Carmen Gloria Quintana with the Sebastian Acevedo Anti-Torture Movement
34

35   Demonstration in front of the National Library

Searching for Colonel Carreno, Santiago

Parents await as police break up high school sit-in

Downtown Santiago

Outside Supreme Court, Santiago

Plaza de Armas, Santiago

41   Funeral for Rodrigo Rojas

Funeral for Father Andre Jarlan, killed by a stray police bullet in La Victoria

Boy wounded after police opened fire in La Victoria

Arrest following flash demonstration for the release of political prisoners, Santiago   44

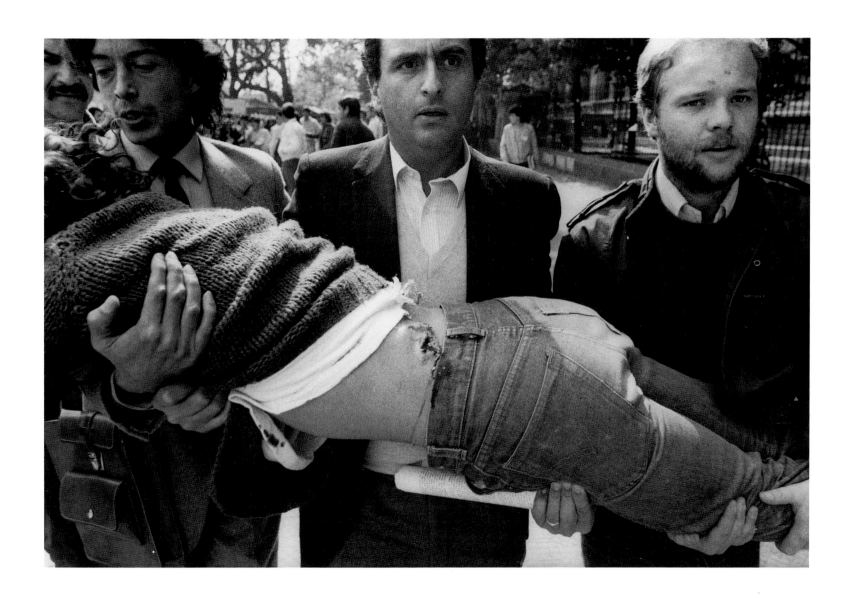

Student wounded during sit-in at the University of Chile

18,000 army troops patrol the
streets of Santiago

La Victoria

La Victoria

"Have you forgotten me?" Figures representing the victims of repression, Santiago

"No more, because there are more of us," International Women's Day, Santiago

Santiago

52

Santiago

General Augusto Pinochet
Ugarte at Diego Portales,
Santiago

Downtown Santiago

55

High school students awaiting President Pinochet, La Ligua

Santiago

Miss Chile pageant, Municipal Theater, Santiago

Santiago

Valparaiso   60

May 1st, Santiago

YES campaign supporter, Santiago

63

NO campaign supporters, Santiago

Last rally for Pinochet prior to plebiscite, Valparaiso

Downtown Santiago

Supporters celebrate triumph of the opposition, Santiago

NO campaign volunteers in bicycle caravan

La Moneda, following results of plebiscite

Military court, downtown Santiago

70

Outside O'Higgins Park, Santiago

MEMORIES OF HOPE
ARIEL DORFMAN

All the material in this text by Ariel Dorfman was written during the Pinochet regime with the exception of the Chronology and the Epilogue, which was written specially for this book.

   The author wishes to thank Maria Angelica, who provided a home away from home all these years, and Howard Goldberg and Maureen Murphy, his editors at The New York Times *and* The Los Angeles Times, *respectively, who labored painfully and loyally to get these words out to the world.*

I know that if I were dead, that is the one night I would want to remember. Too many of those who overflowed the streets in a mad, dazed dance are no longer with us, murdered in the coup and the years that followed. Maybe our dead do remember it: how we roamed downtown Santiago like wild horses in a meadow.

There are certain memories that with the passing of the years become more real than the people who lived them. They're rare memories, different from the common, everyday variety, because you don't wear them out with use. That's the way it was with the night of September 4, 1970. . . . Gonzalo and Felipe stopping perfectly anonymous marchers to force them to join in their song, hugging and congratulating the most absolute strangers. Not one person refused to sing along with them, when asked. Boys and girls who had worked in the campaign until they were ready to fall from exhaustion and had somewhere found the strength to form a dancing chain, boys and girls who, hours later, one hoped, would find themselves tangled up in each other's private arms, bringing the night to an end in the usual not so godly way. Old women, fat from so many beans and so much washing of other people's laundry, holding the hands of their flocks of bewildered, whooping kids. Young workers from the factories sporting little paper hats and plastic horns, as if this were everybody's birthday. . . .

By three, it may have been four, in the morning, we had come to rest our sleepless legs on the high solemn steps of the most powerful bank in Chile, the Banco de Chile. Other couples and even whole families with great-grandfather and their stray dog were already camping out there. Nobody had ever had a picnic on these steps. And nobody knew what Santiago looked like from up here—partly because Santiago had never looked like this before. It was the first time in the history of mankind that any of us—and especially the poor—had been able to explore our own city in this way. I had often noticed how poor people would take long detours not to pass through the center of Santiago, as if they sensed that it was somehow an alien space. But tonight they belonged. I can remember a textile worker sitting on a bench in the Plaza de Armas with his hands behind his neck and his lungs taking in the clean, clear air up there: he felt absolutely at home. I'm not going to move from here, he told us, when we sat down next to him for a minute. I'm going to wait for dawn.

"We're not going to sleep tonight either," Gonzalo told him. "And I know who else isn't going to sleep."

The enemy, of course. To ensure that Gonzalo's as yet unformulated prediction would be fulfilled, a few hours earlier we had driven through the rich neighborhoods of the *barrio alto*, blowing insolent car horns so loudly they would have awakened the dead and certainly those scared-to-death people who had been the lords of Chile's wealth and power and who now mourned Allende's victory behind stony windows.

The enemy must have started to make plans that very night. When we passed by their mansions in Las Condes and Providencia, the latest model cars piled up in front indicated they were having their meetings, too. "Look," I said, still obsessed with the idea of dawns and auroras and mornings, "look, they're conspiring to steal the rays of the sun."

Felipe, whose knowledge was of a more specific, economic nature, suspected less metaphoric intentions. "They'll make a run on the banks," he predicted. "A financial panic, that's what they'll try to create."

But we were oblivious to those dangers. Back in the center, we let our pirate eyes stroll over each bank, really touring Chile itself, each bank bearing the name of a province or of a city, Osorno and La Unión, Valdivia, Banco de Concepción, Llanquihue, as if in there, now Talca, Banco de Curicó, was enclosed, in those giant strongboxes in false Doric style, poor imitations of Paris or New York or Chicago, the country that had been stolen from us for centuries.

The same people kept passing the Banco de Chile again and again, as though they were riders on a merry-go-round or a worn phonograph record. It seemed that, as we could not immediately expropriate the banks, we were going to expropriate each other, and perfect strangers now found themselves dancing the *cueca* together, oh, my Lord, as if they were trying to pound dust out of the marble. If one of the owners of the bank had shown up there by some chance—instead of cowering and conspiring in his *barrio alto* residence—I think we would have stared at him the way you would stare at some leftover, extinct species. To us, they were already relics: bones in a museum, amnesiacs, invisibilities. That's the way Santiago will be, Paula whispered softly, in ten or twenty years. Every person who lives by exploiting others will have gone. . . .

A light fog rolled in as it always did at that hour in Santiago, just before dawn. But for one final, infinite moment, we kept on seeing things as if this fog didn't exist, and the capital lay transformed and clean at our feet.

From: The Last Song of Manuel Sendero *(New York: Viking, 1988), pp. 142–44*

SELECTED CHRONOLOGY, 1970–1982

The italic portions of this chronology were extracted from chronologies prepared by the Congressional Research Service ("Chile, 1960–70: A Chronology"; "Chile Since the Election of Salvador Allende: A Chronology"; "Developments in Chile, March 1973 to the Overthrow of the Allende Government") and from material contained in the June 21, 1973, report of the Senate Foreign Relations Subcommittee on Multinational Corporations entitled "ITT and Chile." The other portions, with the exception of the October 1977 entry, which is from Cultural and Democratic Resistance in Chile Today *(Geneva: IDAC, 1978) are from America's Watch Report, 'Chile Since the Coup: Ten Years of Repression,' August 25, 1983.*

1970

September 4: *Salvador Allende wins 36.3 percent of the vote in the presidential election. Final outcome is dependent on October 24 vote in Congress between Allende and the runner-up, Jorge Alessandri, who received 35.3 percent of the vote. Allende's margin of victory was 39,000 votes out of a total of 3 million votes cast in the election.*

December 21: *President Allende proposes a constitutional amendment establishing state control of the large mines and authorizing expropriation of all foreign firms working them.*

1971

January 28: *40 Committee approves $1,240,000 for the purchase of radio stations and newspapers and to support municipal candidates and other political activities of anti-Allende parties.*

September 28: *President Allende announces that "excess profits" will be deducted from compensation to be paid to nationalized copper companies.*

December 1: *The Christian Democratic and National parties organize the "March of the Empty Pots" by women to protest food shortages.*

1972

January 19: *President Nixon issues a statement to clarify U.S. policy toward foreign expropriation of American interests. The president states that the United States expects compensation to be "prompt, adequate, and effective." The president warns that should compensation not be reasonable, new bilateral economic aid to the expropriating country might* be terminated and the United States would withhold its support from loans under consideration in multi-lateral development banks.

December 4: *Speaking before the General Assembly of the United Nations, President Allende charges that Chile has been the "victim of serious aggression" and adds, "We have felt the effects of a large-scale external pressure against us."*

1973

June 20: *Thousands of physicians, teachers, and students go on strike to protest Allende's handling of the 63-day copper workers' strike.*

July 20: *Truck owners throughout Chile go on strike.*

August 2: *The owners of more than 110,000 buses and taxis go on strike.*

August 23: *General Carlos Prats Gonzalez resigns as*

Allende's defense minister and army commander. *General Pinochet Ugarte is named army commander on August 21. Prats' resignation is interpreted as a severe blow to Allende.*

September 11: *The Chilean military overthrows the government of Salvador Allende. Allende dies during the takeover, reportedly by suicide.*

Decree law no. 1 designates general of the army, Augusto Pinochet Ugarte, president of the Republic of Chile.

Decree law no. 3 declares Chile to be in a state of siege. The traditional safeguards of the judicial courts give way to the expanded power and jurisdiction of the military or special courts.

September 21: Decree law no. 27 dissolves the National Congress.

71 Guards, National Stadium prison camp, Santiago

72 Prisoners, National Stadium prison camp, Santiago

October 8 and November 26: Decree laws no. 76 and no. 145 declare illegal and dissolve parties "with Marxist or related tendencies."

1974

April 22: Decree law no. 463 suspends all other political parties, entities, and groups.

June 14: Decree law no. 521 establishes DINA (Dirección de Inteligencia Nacional), the agency primarily responsible for political arrests and disappearances in Chile.

August: It is estimated that 180,000 people have been detained for periods ranging from a few hours to fourteen months. Of those detained, 1.1 percent go to trial. Selection of prisoners for trial is so arbitrary that prisoners can arrive at trial without being charged with a crime.

August 9: Decree law no. 604 forbids entry into Chile of any person who encourages opinions advocating changing Chile's system of government.

September 16: *President Ford acknowledges covert operations in Chile.*

September 30: The exiled General Carlos Prats—a key constitutionalist leader of the armed forces—and his wife are assassinated in Argentina. Michael Townley, a DINA agent, is later charged with taking part in the car bombing.

December 30: *U.S. military aid is cut off.*

1975

May 4: The government suspends Article 15 of the 1925 Constitution, the constitution then in effect, and extends the period of legal detention from 48 hours to five days "in the case of offenses against the security of the State while a state of emergency is in effect."

73 People arrested after trying to enter Argentine Embassy seeking asylum. Santiago

74 Pablo Neruda's funeral, General Cemetery, Santiago

May 10: Decree law no. 504 authorizes persons detained for political reasons to apply for expulsion, provided an entry visa from another country can be obtained. Approximately 3,500 detainees are given the choice of exile or imprisonment.

June 20: *Pinochet declares there "will be no elections in Chile during my lifetime nor in the lifetime of my successor."*

October 6: Bernardo Leighton—a former vice-president of Chile and a popular Pinochet critic-in-exile—is gunned down in Rome, Italy, in a DINA assassination plot. The attempted assassination leaves Leighton with an egg-size indentation in his skull and partially paralyzes his wife, Anita.

1976

May: An unofficial survey of 200 prisoners (4 percent of whom were minors) at Puchuncavi, an official center, reveals that 88.5 percent had been tortured

75 Outside the morgue, Santiago

physically and that 84 percent had undergone "psychological treatment."

September 21: A car bomb explodes in Washington, D.C., killing Orlando Letelier, an ambassador of the previous government, and Ronni Moffitt, a colleague at the Institute for Policy Studies. Michael Townley later pleads guilty to arranging the bombing on behalf of DINA.

1977

October: For a long time the point at issue was to create an invisible country, a true Chile where one could still touch the not-to-be-remembered past and the not-to-be-dreamed-of future. During this stage, culture was generally clandestine, created on the fringe of everyday life or in its hidden recesses. Such a culture developed spontaneously in the period immediately following the coup d'état and still continues today in the telling of jokes, the spreading of rumors, a few writings; people begin to scribble words on walls, on banknotes, in public lavatories. Illegal journals begin to appear, some slogans on walls, some campaigns of leaflets, books, and reviews printed inside the country, clandestine poetry and painting workshops. The dictatorship's attempts to disperse, to destroy communications, to sow universal mistrust are countered with closer ties, small signs of recognition, the use of language to convey secret messages, the possibility of counter-information. The same tendency can be detected outside the country, in the culture that is going into exile on a mass scale; it is a matter of preserving the national identity somewhere, anywhere, of keeping alive the consciousness and the colors of Chile, of cultivating roots in tiny plots of ground which one day will become common land.

December 27: United Nations criticism provokes Pinochet to decree a national consultation, to be held January 4, 1978, whereby Chileans respond yes or no to whether they support the government against "international aggression." A Chilean flag fills the "yes" box, and the thin ballot paper allows polling officers to see the elector's vote. 75.3 percent vote yes.

1978

March 10: A state of emergency replaces the state of siege. The state of emergency, under international law, allows a state to derogate certain human rights obligations as "required by the exigencies of the situation." The Chilean government alone defines the "exigencies." A state of emergency, though, as a matter of international law, never permits deprivation of life and torture, two nonderogable rights.

June: The Vicaria de la Solidaridad, a Chilean human rights organization , publishes a list of 600 well-documented cases of detainees still missing from the years 1973–1976. . . . The Chilean Commission on Human Rights estimates 1,600–2,500 unresolved disappearances.

December: Fifteen identified bodies, buried in 1975 or 1976, are discovered at an abandoned mine near Lonquen, Chile. For the first time a clear connection is established between the disappearances and murders of persons by government officials.

1980

Thirty-five bodies buried in common graves at Lonquen and Yumbel are identified from lists of missing detainees.

September 11: The government presents the new constitution for a national plebiscite. Public debate is not permitted and official intimidation runs rampant. Chileans adopt the constitution by a large majority.

1981

Expulsions resume after a lapse of three years. The state of emergency authorizes the president to bar Chileans from entering the country if they "constitute a danger to the security of the State." Under transitional provision no. 24 no recourse is available.

March 11: The transitional provision no. 24 authorizes a new administrative system of police control, whereby a Chilean is summarily banished for three months. One who is banished is sent to a remote and isolated area hundreds of miles from home without income or lodging. The resident population is discouraged from lending assistance; the banished must hope that church relief will be available. Judicial internal banishment, where sentences are for longer periods, has also become customary. Approximately 300 Chileans have been banished within the country in two years.

1982

November 8: Pinochet appoints a Special Commission on Exiles. Of the 125 Chileans authorized to return to Chile, 41 are not actually in exile. While this official commission is in existence, two labor leaders are expelled.

. . . NOT TO GET USED TO PINOCHET
NOT TO LET PINOCHET
BECOME A HABIT
PINOCHET MUST BE OUR
NIGHTMARE, NOT OUR
YARDSTICK FOR
MEASURING REALITY.

From: Cultural and Democratic
Resistance in Chile Today.

Hope

My son has been
missing
since May 8
of last year.

    They took him
    just for a few hours
    they said
    just for some routine
    questioning.

After the car left,
the car with no license plate,
we couldn't

    find out

anything else
about him.

But now things have changed.
We heard from a compañero
who just got out
that five months later
they were torturing him
in Villa Grimaldi,
at the end of September
they were questioning him
in the red house
that belonged to the Grimaldis.

    They say they recognized
    his voice his screams
    they say.

Somebody tell me frankly
what times are these
what kind of world
what country?
What I'm asking is
how can it be
that a father's
joy
a mother's
joy
is knowing
that they
that they are still
torturing
their son?
Which means
that he was alive
five months later
and our greatest
hope
will be to find out
next year
that they're still torturing him
eight months later

and he may might could
still be alive.

From: Last Waltz in Santiago *(New York:
Viking Penguin, 1988).*

September 11, 1983. Santiago

Returning to Chile after 10 years of forced exile, I am shocked by all that has changed. I am also shocked by what remains the same. . . .

I had read that General Augusto Pinochet's model of development had created a new and opulent social class, but nothing could prepare me for what I felt when, after passing through a virtually unaltered Santiago, I reached the *barrio alto*—the hill-slope neighborhood where the privileged classes of Chile traditionally reside. This is the only part of the city that is unrecognizable. I found myself being guided, like a tourist, along unknown avenues filled with hundreds of glass towers and shopping malls, splendid gardens and efficient freeways. I could not believe that this was Chile. It was as if I had stepped into one of the nicer suburbs of a metropolis back in the States. In just 10 years, a modernized, sleek, and exclusive city-in-itself had arisen, as if from nowhere.

There has always been, in Chile as in the rest of Latin America, an abysmal distance between the rich and the poor. But those who live in these countries find ways of disguising that distance or ignoring it. My years away from home have given back to me not only the possibility of measuring that distance but of overwhelming me with the stark, irrefutable evidence of its malignant growth. Only a few miles from the *barrio alto* is the price that Chile must pay for so much ostentatious luxury for a few: the slums where millions of impoverished Chileans live in squalor. When I left Chile, these people had been poor. When I came back, I discovered that General Pinochet had performed the considerable miracle of making them even more miserable, stranding them even further from the mainstream of society.

Visiting one shantytown, I realized that these people have lived an exile more terrible than my own. They may have had the comfort of the mountains, and they could speak Spanish while I had to learn foreign languages and read incomprehensible street signs, but they have been turned into strangers in their own land. They have not only been defined a decent life but also the means to protest against that denial.

What is true of them is true of most Chileans, even those in a better financial situation. It is as if Chile had been struck by a plague. I am scandalized by the physical ruin of my country. The economic crisis, the worst in our history, touches everybody.

I drove through the industrial belt of Santiago and it was like visiting a ghost town. Stores are empty. Most of my friends and family are unemployed or hold only part-time jobs. Though it is winter, there is no heating in the house where I am living: Money must be used for more urgent matters.

And yet, in this land without a free press, this land where hundreds of thousands have been jailed and humiliated, where exile and violence and lying have become as natural as breathing air, the predominant mood is not despair. People know, of course, that General Pinochet still holds power. He can still order his troops to murder, and he does. He can still torture, and does. He can still transmit his most incoherent thoughts into each home whenever he so desires, and he so desires incessantly. But a dictator cannot last unless he rules the minds, as well as the bodies, of his people. If he cannot make their dreams coincide with his promises, and their fears coincide with his threats, he is lost.

From "An Exile Finds Chile 'Struck by a Plague,'" New York Times, September 11, 1983.

. . . How to govern a country which is in ruins? When there is a democratic system again, there will be no pressure for the poor people to swallow their demands. They have starved. They have lost their health and welfare benefits. They need employment and a drastic rise in wages. With the economy in a shambles, how to give them a much-needed larger part of the cake, when the middle classes and the entrepreneurs are also in need of assistance and guarantees that there will be an orderly transition?

It is, of course, that very economic devastation which has eroded what was left of Pinochet's popularity. Over a third of the nation's work force is unemployed, and many of those who do work are in the Minimum Employment Plan, engaged in barren jobs for $25 a month. It is heart-wrenching. Everywhere I went, I saw able-bodied men and women laboring at public gardens, carrying stones from one side of the road to the other or simply, and quite uselessly, sweeping the dust and watching it settle. "We don't even get enough money to pay for the bus," one of them told me, but his eyes were not downcast. "At least we can make believe we are active."

Priests who live in the slums have calculated that nearly 70 percent of their congregations are jobless. When I asked one man how he managed, he cheerfully elucidated: he paid no utility bills. He stole the electricity with a wire, and had methods for stopping the needles that marked the water and the gas. Santiago is covered with roving salesmen, hawking all sorts of unnecessary artifacts and trinkets, toys, and flags, even herbs and plants. In the open-air market, I saw men selling cigarettes one by one.

The middle classes are desperate. They believed in Pinochet's promise of an economic "miracle" and were only too willing to overlook the human rights atrocities while they could enjoy the short-lived boom of a couple of years ago. Under Milton Friedman's dictates, imported articles flooded Chile—ravaging the national industry—and everybody started buying consumer goods on credit. Now, with the crisis, they cannot pay for them, and the result is an accelerating chain of bankruptcies. (A lawyer friend with contacts in the government told me that before the coup, the bankruptcy applications at any given moment could have fit into a drawer. Now the four walls of a special room are crammed full of files and a special law has been decreed to speed the process up.)

Engineers have opened restaurants. Architects are selling eggs. I know a dentist who gathers wood in the hills to heat his house in the winter. After midnight, I have seen whole families scurrying with their furniture out of their houses, moving so they will not have to pay the past six months' rent, leaving no forwarding address. Although many high-rises and shopping malls have gone up in the rich neighborhoods, they are beginning to deteriorate. Nobody is buying. Perhaps the symbol of all this is an ultramodern ice-skating rink which I visited. It is now abandoned and all that is left is a slush of dirty, melted water where the Chilean bourgeoisie once dreamt of figures of eight on a white expanse of imported ice.

From: "Chile Is a Swing," Village Voice, *November 15, 1983.*

September 11, 1984

Bethesda, Md.—For 11 years, each time I have turned on the radio, it has been with the hope that the next bulletin would report that Chile's ruler, General Augusto Pinochet, has been overthrown. . . .

Yet, he has survived. Many critics who a year ago believed he was doomed now expect that he may misrule Chile until the end of the millennium. Apparently sharing that perception, the general recently went so far as to publicly compare himself to a Roman emperor.

How to get rid of the two-bit emperor?

The answer of most Chileans has been, until now, fundamentally nonviolent. It is true that some fringe groups on the extreme left advocate armed struggle, and also true that the strong Communist Party, which for 60 years had sustained the idea that socialism could be reached without use of force, has proclaimed the right of public insurrection. But in practice the Communists have not engaged in any significant acts of armed resistance. They are held back, I believe, not only by the intuition that such a course might prove suicidal but also by the hope of most people, their own militants included, that change can come about without a prolonged civil war like El Salvador's.

The typical attitude is that of hundreds of thousands who the other day stopped at noon to sing "Thanks to Life," a song by Latin America's greatest folk artist, the Chilean Violeta Parra. This is the Chileans' answer: despite having been raped, we do not want to reply with more pain and death. If there is any Latin American country where active nonviolence has deep roots in history and national character, it is Chile. . . . There is still a chance that my long wait by the radio will not prove futile. Augusto Pinochet remains in power only because he confronts a divided opposition and is supported by a united army. If the situation were reversed, he might find that the emperor he incarnates is not his namesake Augustus Caesar, as he must believe, but Augustus's great-grandson Caligula, who was eliminated by his pretorian guard.

From: "Roman Emperor Pinochet Must Go," New York Times, *September 11, 1984.*

September 18, 1984

. . . What he decided to do was to leave Chile under his false identity. He settled in Argentina for a couple of months and officially asked the junta to allow him to return. This seemed a plausible solution—many exiles were being given permission to come back home under an uncertain *apertura*, or opening, promised by Pinochet. But as tension mounted, the government cracked down again, internally and externally. Among the thousands of permissions denied was Gazmuri's.

He could have gone back under his clandestine name as he had so many times. Instead, he chose to make his right to return legally to his own land a test case.

Along with five other major political figures in exile, he boarded an Air France plane in Buenos Aires, sending ahead the message that they were on their way.

After crossing the Andes, they were unable to leave the plane. A group of plainclothesmen blocked the exit. The exiles insisted on descending and being prosecuted legally if they had committed some crime. The Chilean authorities would not hear of it and ordered the plane back to Buenos Aires. Many tense hours passed. Human rights organizations presented two writs of habeas corpus to the Santiago judiciary: When these were finally rejected, the plane got ready for takeoff.

The exiles passively resisted, lying down in the aisles. Members of Pinochet's secret police then boarded the plane, roughed them up, and handcuffed them to the seats. They stayed on the flying prison until it landed again in Buenos Aires.

The exiles stubbornly returned on the next flight to Chile—where they were dispatched just as promptly, with a one-way ticket to Bogota, Colombia. When they bought a ticket back to Chile, the Pinochet government threatened the Colombian airline with a fine and, possibly, revoking its license to fly to Santiago. And to make sure that no other refugees around the world repeated the strategy, it sent a confidential memo to all airlines (including several in America that serve Chile) listing 4,942 people who should not be embarked.

Not content with having violated every human right imaginable, Pinochet has now invented a new "crime": Not only are certain Chileans refused entry to their own land, they cannot even board a plane with that destination.

From: "Will U.S. Airlines Do Pinochet's Bidding?" Los Angeles Times, September 18, 1984.

February 18, 1985. Santiago

Old legends are still told in the Chilean countryside. One legend explains what happens when a child disappears: he has been kidnapped by witches, and his captors, to insure his servitude, break all his bones, sew together different parts of his body and turn his head around so he must always look and walk backward. His eyes, ears, and mouth are constantly stitched up. The creature is called an Imbunche.

There is no way of knowing if General Augusto Pinochet ever heard that tale when he was young, but there can be no doubt that he has done everything in his power to turn each Chilean, and Chile itself, into an Imbunche.

Chileans do not know, cannot know, if today their voices will be overheard, if tomorrow their bodies will be fractured. But even if they are not arrested or beaten up by the police or thrown out of work, they are, in a way, already like Imbunches. They are isolated from each other, their means of communicating suppressed, their connections cut off, their senses blocked by fear.

From: "A Rural Chilean Legend Come True," New York Times, February 18, 1985.

April 13, 1985

Among the many telegrams Ronald Reagan received on November 7, 1984, one offered the congratulations of Chile's ruler, General Augusto Pinochet. At the very moment, perhaps, that hands in Washington were opening that message, a raid was being conducted by 30 Chilean secret police agents on an apartment in Santiago where, for the previous few months, a loose coalition of democratic socialist parties known as the Bloque Socialista, or Socialist Bloc, had been meeting. In similar raids all over Santiago, dozens of dissidents were being rounded up and interrogated.

The raiders were not only interested in the opposition leaders; they had also come for the booty. They stole the typewriters, the telephone, the furniture, the lamps, even the toilet paper—anything that could be converted into cash. Except for the man in charge of the operation, apparently an army captain, they all wore ski masks. Later, they did not have to worry about concealing their identities because the prisoners' eyes were taped.

An old friend of mine, Lucho Alvarado, was one of the opposition leaders in the apartment that day. It was his second arrest. After President Salvador Allende was murdered, in the coup of September 11, 1973, Alvarado went underground. There was reason to suspect that the military might arrest him. He had directed a public agency that provided housing for the poor and, in the last desperate months of Allende's government, had worked in the presidential palace, helping to organize against the impending military takeover. But after three weeks in hiding, he risked coming home. A half-hour after he returned, just as he was coming out of the shower, a gang of policemen burst into his house and carried him off to the National Stadium, where thousands of others were being held. Like most of them, he was tortured for days and then shipped to Chacabuco, a concentration camp in the northern desert, first in the stinking hold of a ship, then by train. IHe was freed nine months later. Charges were never pressed against him. When they picked him up eleven years later, he recalled with astonishment that he had arrived in Chacabuco on November 7, 1973.

This time, however, Alvarado was not tortured. His face was hooded and he was insulted by his guards, but as soon as he arrived in the cellars of the National Information Center, Pinochet's secret police agency (formerly DINA), he noticed a hesitancy on the part of his captors. This did not allay his fears; he knew that in this same place people had spent infernal months of horror, only to disappear forever or have their bodies dumped, mutilated, in some river or on some street. But the interrogation was courteous, almost conversational. This, he thought, might be a tactic to put him off balance. But five days later, when he was placed on a bus heading south, he knew he would not end up in a concentration camp. He was about to become a *relegado*, an internal exile. He was not told his destination; finally he arrived at the small fishing village of Chonchi, on the island of Chiloé, 800 miles south of Santiago.

Alvarado's banishment was part of an offensive that General Pinochet had been threatening for months. The previous year, pressured by a mounting opposition movement and besieged by an economic crisis which had alienated vast sectors of hitherto loyal middle-class supporters, he had been forced to grant some concessions. Opposition magazines circulated, full of stories about the regime's corruption and its human rights abuses, and democratic parties surfaced. Elections were held in several trade unions, professional organizations, and student associations, all of them won by candidates representing forces that demanded that the government resign. The police seemed unable to dislodge groups of homeless migrants from the countryside who had taken over some of the city's vacant lots. People were being beaten up, shantytowns raided, hundreds of slum dwellers shot by police on days when protests and strikes were scheduled. Democratic leaders were harassed, waylaid on streets, threatened. Even though factions of the opposition movement could not agree on a common strategy, they managed to organize a general strike, on October 30, which paralyzed the country.

The situation was getting out of hand. There was an alarming rise in bombings—some undoubtedly perpetrated by groups associated with the Communist Party but a larger number carried out by police provocateurs seeking to create a sense of chaos which would frighten the middle class and pave the way for a crackdown. For some time, Pinochet had been warning his adversaries that there would be a "second September 11." His invocation of the coup that brought him to power was an admission that he had not solved the country's basic problems and could offer only another bloodbath.

There has been no bloodbath—at least not yet. After Pinochet proclaimed the state of siege, on November 6, his brutality consisted of selective blows that left the opposition gasping for air. It was a toned-down reiteration of the violence of 11 years before. Instead of widespread torture, massive executions and bombings, and hundreds of disappearances,

there were a few deaths, short-term abductions, frequent beatings, and periodic raids. Instead of killing journalists, Pinochet issued a decree shutting down magazines. Instead of arresting the most visible leaders of the parties, those who had contacts abroad, the authorities concentrated on their seconds-in-command, cutting off the leaders from the people. Why use the enormous National Stadium when a smaller one was just as good? Chileans remember the September coup so vividly that the government could evoke a Pavlovian response with a few dramatic gestures, terrorizing and demobilizing a majority of the people. (The brutal murder of three prominent opposition figures shortly before this article went to press indicates that the gestures may get more dramatic, and dangerous, in the days to come.)

"This is going to be a Polish solution," a high-level official confided to a group of reporters, without a hint of irony in his voice. "A lot of control and not much spectacle. Nothing for foreign TV news to cover." Such a solution had the added benefit of appeasing the forces that viewed the state of siege as excessive and whose support Pinochet needed to remain in power: the U.S. government, which had been pressing for a dialogue between the military and center-right members of the opposition, and elements in the army and the ruling elite who hoped to enlist the cooperation of the opposition Christian Democrats in a gradual transition to a limited democracy which would outlaw the Marxists and their allies. More violence also would have brought the already tense relations with the Catholic Church to the breaking point.

Internal exile is a pillar of this strategy. It has immense advantages for the dictatorship. It disrupts and neutralizes the dissident movement by sending some of its most militant members to faraway places, where they lose contact with what is going on. The whole country becomes a prison, and it costs the state nothing. The government does not need to put the offenders on trial; it does not need to open new jails or overcrowd already filled penitentiaries. It does not even need to feed the exiles, who must work to support their families and themselves. The secret detention centers are kept conveniently transitory, way stations where people can be quickly "treated" before being dispatched elsewhere. Nor are the effects on the permanent inhabitants of those remote places to be overlooked: there, for all to see, is proof of the government's omnipotence. Plus the side effects: *relegados* lose their jobs; if they are students, their careers are ruined.

To the Chilean military, *relegación* represents a superb use of the local terrain. Around 40 years ago the writer Benjamin Subercaseaux called Chile's geography *loca* ("crazy"). Now that very craziness is being used by quite sane rulers to fragment and isolate their subjects. The country is almost 3,000 miles long and at no point more than 220 miles wide, with great extremes in climate, from desert to arctic, a Mediterranean-like central region and an Oregon-like southern forest and lake district. What has been the delight of poets, nature lovers, adventurers, geologists, and geographers is also, unfortunately, made to order for General Pinochet.

From: "Return to a Country of Exiles,"
The Nation, *April 13, 1985.*

November 23, 1985

"Tenemos las manos limpias!" "Our hands are clean!" These words have become the rallying cry for thousands of Chileans in recent months as they attempt to rid themselves of the dictatorship with which General Augusto Pinochet has been oppressing them for 12 years.

Students shout these words and show their hands in the streets, just before the police descend upon them with nightsticks and water cannons. Imprisoned trade union leaders write these words in manifestos sent from jail. At the end of performances, actors display their hands, open, clean, palms out, to the spectators, who answer by lifting their own arms. At funerals for slum dwellers killed in raids, mourners expose their untainted hands to those who line avenues and watch them file by.

What they are saying is that they have never murdered anyone, that they have never tortured anyone, that they have not exiled anyone, have not thrown people out of work, have not starved children, have not ruined the country, are not responsible for accumulating the largest per capita debt in the world. They are saying that the hands that are clean should be the hands that should govern the country, that should vote, that should be given the chance to rebuild the raped land and heal the wounds of the past.

The Pinochet regime does not seem to be heeding their call. Since its inception, it has always tried to present itself as immaculate. I remember that one of the first decrees of the military junta, after it overthrew the elected president, Salvador Allende, in 1973, was to order that all walls should be painted white. At the very moment when football stadiums were being converted into concentration camps, the streets of Santiago were full of soldiers and often civilians washing away the graffiti, the political slogans, the mutlicolored murals from the walls. Chile's new rulers were not only cleaning up the city and erasing the past but subconsciously, I believe, whitewashing themselves in advance, hiding the blood that was still to come. Perhaps they thought the blood could always remain concealed and they would never be held accountable.

Now those hands of death stand accused by the hands of life. Now the hands of life are demanding that the truth of these 12 years of sorrow be made public. The hands of life are saying that the nation can never be at peace unless those who committed the crimes are judged and measures are taken to insure that such revolting acts can never be repeated.

How is this to happen? Those hands that are unpolluted also happen to be empty and weaponless. How are the hands of life to convince those whose hands are bloody to step down and be sentenced? Until now, the opposition's uneasy answer has been to mobilize the people, show that they have the capacity to paralyze the country, and, by making it ungovernable, force enough military officers to come to their senses and initiate a transition to democracy before it is too late.

There is a slim chance this strategy might just work. Two months ago, a large number of opposition forces representing the vast majority of Chileans signed an accord that established, among other things, the way in which the military would be judged for human rights abuses under a future democratic regime. Uniformed individuals who had committed crimes would be prosecuted, but there would be no special tribunals for that purpose, nor an overall purge of the armed forces.

Millions of Chileans have signed that agreement. I signed, like many others, even though I felt a Nuremberg-type trial that would investigate the military and uncover the deep causes of our national tragedy would be exceptionally important for Chile's future—that we must, for our own sanity, bring to the surface all the atrocities hidden all these years behind the supposedly unsoiled walls.

But I also recognize that to purge ourselves totally of the forces of violence, we would have to achieve a total military victory against our rulers—we would have to launch and win an armed insurrection against them.

Most Chileans reject the solution—partly, I suppose, out of realism, since this would be suicidal. But there are deeper moral reasons for avoiding an armed confrontation with the military. We have been raped, humiliated, excluded—and yet, if humanly possible, we do not want to get our hands bloody in order to reach democracy. We do not want to do to our executioners what they did to us.

But there is a limit to patience. Let it be remembered, in the future, that if we are forced to resort to other methods to liberate ourselves, we wanted our hands to remain clean.

From: "In Chile, a Show of Hands," New York Times, *November 23, 1985.*

July 9, 1986

There used to be a time when people in Chile, upon taking leave of each other, would utter a simple "goodbye."

I found the words curiously changed: "*Que estes bien*," people said: "Hope you'll be all right."

A subconscious way, perhaps, for those who have lived almost 13 years under the dictatorship of General Augusto Pinochet to express their vulnerability, the feeling that they cannot really be certain something terrible won't happen soon to the person they're talking to.

And so the last words I was ever to say to 19-year-old Rodrigo Rojas De Negri as he departed my home in Santiago on June 26 after a visit were the automatic, "Hope you'll be all right."

Six days later, on the morning of July 2, he and a friend, Carmen Quintana, after having been beaten by soldiers whose faces were covered with black combat paint, were sprayed with a flammable liquid and set afire. Death has a way of arriving unannounced to young people. How was I to guess that within a week Rodrigo would be dead?

How I regret now that the last time he came to visit we did not talk at length. But he saw I was busy and departed quickly, after a brief chat. We promised to see each other next week, at least before I left for Washington, so I could carry news of how he was doing to his exiled mother, Veronica De Negri, a friend from the times when I myself had been an exile in the United States.

Veronica was a torture victim of the Chilean regime who, presumably because of her work with Amnesty International, had been prohibited from returning to her native land. Having waited in vain for nine years to come back with his whole family, Rodrigo had finally chosen to return on his own, eager to explore the country of his origins and figure out where his true identity lay. It is, of course, risky for anybody to return to Chile, but who could have anticipated such a savage homecoming?

We are a peaceful nation with a longstanding democratic tradition. How long are we to tolerate this horror? Must a thousand Rodrigos die as the price we pay for getting back our country?

From: "Hope You'll Be All Right,"
Washington Post, *July 9, 1986.*

September 8, 1986. Durham, N.C.

The failed guerrilla attempt on the life of General Augusto Pinochet on Sunday, almost 13 years to the day that he seized power in a bloody coup in Chile, marks a turning point in the history of my country.

It is not the violence that is new. We have had more than our fill of that. In fact, given the systematic violation of human rights, the murder and exile of thousands of dissidents, the arrest and torture of hundreds of thousands of others, what is puzzling is not that such an attempt should have been made but that it did not come sooner. General Pinochet, after all, is merely reaping the destruction he himself has sown.

What is new is that the hopes for a peaceful transition to democracy seem to have been dashed. Despite the death that had been visited upon us, despite the disastrous economic situation, an overwhelming majority of Chileans stubbornly clung to the expectation—and we continue to do so against all odds today—that we would be able to return our land to civilized rule using nonviolent means.

We kept anticipating that, unless the government took effective steps to hold elections and give the people back its sovereignty, the country would be inevitably split apart and lapse into a generalized confrontation.

General Pinochet's intransigent decision to remain in power until 1997, his invasion of the slum areas, the impoverishment of vast sectors of a country where unemployment runs at about 30 percent—all created fertile ground for action by those dissidents who were losing patience. Many of them, basically linked to the powerful Communist Party, had gradually come to the conclusion that only armed resistance to an army at war with its own people could bring the dictatorship down.

Most Chileans, including myself, saw this call to arms as suicidal and irresponsible. We argued that this polarization of the country into two military bands could only strengthen the stranglehold that General Pinochet has on his army and allow him to present himself as the only man who could save the country from a Communist takeover.

Things have turned out, unfortunately, just as we predicted. The general is now able to proclaim a state of siege, jailing his main opponents, including many who have resolutely proclaimed nonviolence as the only method of struggle. If knowledge of how he has acted in the past is worth anything, he will probably continue mass arrests until he has wiped out all the organizations that have been peacefully mounting a campaign of civil disobedience against him during the last month, including a successful general strike two months ago.

But these measures will not solve Chile's problems—because it is General Pinochet himself who is at the root of Chile's problems. Thirteen years ago, he promised to wipe out Marxism. He has only driven a Communist Party that did not believe in belligerence to become a vast network for armed resistance. He has turned a country that for most of its history was fundamentally harmonious and participatory into a place where the young learn violence every day—in the streets that are patrolled by marauding soldiers, in the schools where they are expelled and beaten up, in the lack of employment and the abundance of hunger.

More violence will beget more violence.

Is it already too late?

From: "Pinochet Has Reaped What He Has Sown," New York Times, *September 8, 1986.*

October 18, 1986

General Augusto Pinochet . . . went wild. This was the pretext he had been waiting for to crush an opposition that had been mounting a campaign of protracted civil disobedience against him. He declared a state of siege, shut down six magazines and a couple of news agencies, raided shantytowns, expelled foreign priests. His secret policemen picked up a number of prominent dissidents. Some of those were lucky. They were carted off to an official jail—paradoxically, one of the only secure places to be if the death squads are also out to get you. Others were arrested by men without warrants, and their bodies, riddled with bullets, began turning up several days later all over Santiago. . . .

The horror was compounded by its familiarity: it was as if we were all caught up, one more time, in the endless repetition of the 1973 coup. The terror was widespread. When I called on the phone, my friends did not answer. They had gone into hiding. It was enough for the police to be hunting an undetermined 500 to induce thousands of others to leave home, sleeping in their clothes at night, just in case. Carrasco had been taken out in his underwear. "Don't put on your shoes," they had said to him. "You won't be needing them." Suddenly, to the new despair about what was happening to my country was added the old, bitter feeling of impotence that had haunted the long years of my exile, before Pinochet had allowed me to return home: a funeral is being held, a boot is breaking down the door to your friend's house, a woman in a slum who gave you tea is watching troops shatter her windows and bayonet her mattress, a priest who stood in front of tanks to stop a raid is being put on a plane while his parishioners sing at the airport so that at least he will be able to hear them one last time. If there was at least something you could do. . . .

The next day, however, when a reporter from United Press International called to inform me in Durham, North Carolina, that a wire dispatched from Buenos Aires had just announced that one of the other corpses found in Chile had now been identified and was none other than my own, I was brutally reminded that distance from one's country when a dictator rules is not only a curse; it can also confer the ambiguous relief of safety.

From "Reports of My Death," The Nation, *October 18, 1986.*

October 6, 1987

There is no ending in sight, however, happy or of any other sort, for Chile itself.

. . . the mood of the country is despondent, if not despairing. Since an economic crisis had weakened the government in 1982 and drained most of its middle-class support, the opposition's strategy had been to mobilize a grassroots coalition that, engaging in demonstrations and civil disobedience, would make the country so ungovernable that the military would be forced to negotiate a transition to democracy. Those plans have been, for the most part, shelved. Nobody I spoke to on this occasion believes Pinochet can be overthrown in the near future. What looms unavoidably on the horizon is an upcoming plebiscite, to be held before 1989, in which the citizens will be allowed to say yes or no to the candidate that the armed forces will name—in all likelihood, the general himself, who, if confirmed, would then serve out another eight years as president. Even if he loses he will retain his command over the army and veto power over any other government elected.

The prospects are therefore dismal. It is unthinkable that Pinochet could lose a referendum in which his government registers the voters, prepares the ballots, counts them, investigates irregularities, judges appeals against its own decisions. When I went to register to vote, for instance, I discovered several well-fed, soldierlike young men ahead of me on line. I knew the armed forces had already been registering their men in the barracks. How could I tell if they were being registered now, as rumors have it, for a second, for a third time? Is anybody going to allow me into the barracks to review their names? In a country where terror and intimidation have continued unabated for the last 14 years? In a country where an old worker tells me that he is not sure if someone will not photograph him when he is voting, where a slum dweller informs me that she will get the roof to her hut only after Pinochet is elected?

But fraud is not the only trick up the general's sleeve. There is a worse scenario: he could win the election simply by default. If he can register the 19 percent of the country that supports him, according to his own opinion polls, and dissuade the rest from voting, he will not need to cheat. This is not as implausible as it sounds. In order to vote, one must first procure a new identity card, a relatively expensive endeavor for the 60 percent of the population who are living in extreme poverty. Many poor people with whom I spoke told me they had neither the money nor the time to waste. "I can feed my children for six days on what it takes to get that card," a woman on the minimum employment plan ($25 a month for weeding public gardens) whispered to me. "And all for what?"

The divided, fragmented opposition groups do not seem to have a clear answer to her question. They are even now bickering among themselves as to how they should confront the plebiscite. The bulk of the opposition, in the center and the left, have called for massive voter registration, in the hope that if a large number of citizens are on the rolls, the army will realize that Pinochet cannot possibly be elected and will withdraw his candidacy and agree to free, pluralistic elections. But the Communist Party has denounced such efforts as legitimizing structures that are immoral and unfair and over which people have no real control. This is not the only matter splitting the anti-Pinochet forces. Should the parties set up legal organizations adhering to a law which they themselves regard as antidemocratic? The Christian Democrats, Chile's largest party, which recently tilted rightward at its national convention, have decided to legalize their party officially, arguing this is the only way they can exercise some control over the plebiscite. The diverse socialist groups reject this tactic, saying that this is playing into Pinochet's hands. The only hopeful sign of unity is among the youth organizations: 11 of them issued a unique ultimatum to their elders, telling them that if they did not start working together, the new generation was going to take matters into its own hands.

Behind these discussions, there is a major question

that invariably crops up at the moment when any dictatorship is seeking to establish more permanent structures of repression: What limits should be placed on one's participation in a legal system which one rejects? Is it better to abstain? Or is it better to uncomfortably sabotage the system from within?

And yet, I would give the wrong impression if I suggested that these debates were raging feverishly all over the country. To the contrary, I found most of the people absorbed in their own precarious survival, extracting whatever morsel of satisfaction they could from the privacy of their hidden lives, tending to mistrust the idea that things will ever change. Even many friends who agreed that it was necessary to register to vote so Pinochet would be forced to commit fraud and could at least be denied legitimacy in his next term admitted that they had not yet done so. "Will it really make a difference?", people kept asking themselves.

I found a similar weariness in the streets. One day I stopped, in the center of town, to watch something which was not new to me: an eight-year-old girl surrounded by 30–40 spectators. She dipped a rag in paraffin, lit it with a match, put out the fire by swallowing the rag, repeated the operation until a man in the crowd signaled her to cease—a few pesos had been deposited in a hat on the ground. The group dispersed as if nothing had happened, as if what they had just witnessed were normal. Perhaps they knew that the girl was at least going to eat that day—others her age are less fortunate.

It was that profound apathy I found most disturbing on this trip. For years, the anti-Pinochet forces have been fighting to get a newspaper published. Since March of this year, two opposition dailies have been coming out, and I had expected them both, in a land where an overwhelming majority of the people abhor the government, to be doing splendidly. Not at all. I visited one of them. The dictatorship is trying to strangle it financially and has hit it with a lawsuit for having published an ad signed and paid for by a group of prominent Communists. "If they fine us $40,000, as well they may," one of the editors told me, "we may have to close." But what really worried him was that the paper was not selling enough copies.

"People frankly don't think that more information will change their lives," a psychologist friend said to me the night I arrived. "It's easier to close your eyes and not believe anything."

Two days before we had returned to Chile, four urban guerrillas escaped from a penitentiary in Valparaiso. I thought that this sort of exploit would be greeted by most people, whether they agreed with the revolutionaries or not, as a cause for glee; confessions had been extracted from these men by the most unspeakable torture, and, besides, the government was looking extremely foolish and inefficient. But the automatic reaction I encountered most of the time I was there was of utter suspicion. People did not assume that the evasion had even taken place: here was one more deception being staged by the military to get rid of their enemies. One of my friends, a Catholic priest, reminded me that Chile has turned into a country where you cannot even believe the clouds in the sky.

From: "Exile's Return," Village Voice, *October 6, 1987.*

September 11, 1988. Santiago

. . . Pinochet announced the lifting of the state of emergency that had served as the legal instrument with which he had been able to arbitrarily exile citizens for the last 15 years. I saw the measure as most people in Chile saw it: a temporary abrogation, designed to persuade the voters, who must decide on October 5 whether to say yes or no to eight more years of his rule, that the general had quite suddenly suffered a miraculous conversion and become democratic. True, we were overjoyed at the return of those exiles able to afford a quick ticket home. And we raucously celebrated the fact that the government, in principle, could no longer operate outside the law, dissidents could not be sent into internal exile, publications could not be banned nor public rallies forbidden. . . .

General Pinochet's temporary and cosmetic liberalization is born out of his need to be nationally and internationally legitimized as Chile's ruler in an election considered fair and clean. This is an absurd pretension. One month of restored freedoms does not blot out 15 years of incessant terror. There is no equality of opportunities between the leaders of the opposition—with their scant resources, their innumerable intimidated supporters, their memories of constant harassment—and a government that still despotically controls the police, the television stations, the streets, the many levers of the economy, the subsidies for housing and nutrition and jobs and schools.

And yet, for all our misgivings, this opening is an extremely hopeful sign. It is possible that Pinochet has persuaded some voters that he has changed his spots. But the major effect is to diminish the fear that was the source and sustenance of his power for so long. Even before these psuedo-benevolent measures were announced, most of the public opinion polls showed the Vote No campaign winning the plebiscite handily.

Even so, what worries us most, of course, is what will happen after October 5. Several army commanders and General Pinochet himself have threatened the citizenry, if we, dare to vote no, with a repetition of the same repression of 1973, when they overthrew the constitutional government. What is to stop him from reversing his present liberalization because the Fatherland is in danger?

Pressure from the international community may well prove decisive if the military government tries to commit fraud the day of the plebiscite or to deny the triumph of the opposition that very night. A pariah, almost a global leper, Pinochet craves foreign recognition. People and governments abroad who care about the future of democracy and stability in my land should remain watchful. But vigilance from outside Chile will be effective only if inside the country our citizens are ready to stand up for their rights when, once again, as must inevitably happen as soon as the dictator feels threatened, he tries to take back what he so ungraciously and clumsily conceded for electoral reasons.

The general, naturally, insists that if he is not elected, the result will be chaos, death and disintegration.

From: "A Holiday for Exiles in Chile," Los Angeles Times, *September 11, 1988.*

October 4, 1988

. . . For the first time in my many visits to Chile, I felt something different. No matter how magnificent and defiant their activities had been in the past, they were always tinged by a hint of futility or even despair. It was as if deep down the dissidents knew that they were not really affecting the destiny of their country, but performing a symbolic act of discontent. I had watched and participated in countless street protests—where the opposition staged raucous calls for change—a morality play directed at bystanders who were too scared to join in or at the armed forces who were too walled-in to listen. No matter how inspiring those protests were—and they had not given Pinochet one day's rest to stabilize his rule—there was an abstraction to them, a ritualistic, circular quality that ended up tiring the protesters as well as the police, because they seemed to lead nowhere except to the reiterated statement, *We are here and we will not go away*. I had heard large groups of activists shouting the ambiguous impersonal cry, *Y va a caer* (and he's gonna fall), without anybody ever stopping to spell out who exactly was going to do the pushing.

The opponents I saw in the training session, and in any number of activities for the NO, had imperceptibly changed. The multiple needs that come out of the electoral process have given them an astonishing concreteness and immediacy, their energies channeled into urgent tasks that cannot be postponed. I found every one of my friends doing something for the campaign, which does not mean that the old habits have died out. I went to a meeting of Professionals for the NO, where 2,000 activists lost three or four hours listening to songs as beautiful as they were numerous, speeches as full of fire as they were unnecessary, and infinite declarations of support from organizations that everybody knew were for the NO vote. It may have been my years in the pragmatic United States, but I felt that our time could have been better employed by quickly sending those present out to convince voters. Or could it be that my years in exile have separated me from my compañeros in Chile who require the comfort of their own company, the certainty of identity and belonging that rites like these bestow, and that help them to conquer, one more weary time, the fear that even the most valiant know is lurking inside? But even in self-referential acts such as that one, there was an anticipation of a new Chile, where the opposition would not be isolated by fear, where millions of Chileans would go beyond the passive act of simply watching the struggle from the sidewalks, and become, finally, in however limited a fashion, protagonists of their own fate. The slogan of the NO campaign is *La alegria viene* (joy is on its way).

From: "Reports from the Heart of the NO," Village Voice, October 4, 1988.

October 18, 1988. Santiago

It was the sudden darkness that awoke me hours before dawn on October 5, the day the Chilean people were to vote yes or no to eight more years of General Augusto Pinochet's rule. Like so many of our fellow countrymen, my wife Angélica and I had found it difficult to fall asleep. We had ample reason to be concerned.

Santiago, Chile's capital, was flooded with rumors. It was murmured that Pinochet had finally been informed by his fawning ministers—who up till then had been assuring him of total success—that he would lose the next day's election. If that were so, a coup might be imminent. Or the general might wait for the results, announcing only those favorable to him, claim victory, and then black out the country, take over the opposition radio stations, and when protesters filled the streets either repress them savagely or have the secret police infiltrate the crowds and create a riot which would allow him to suspend the electoral process. As we tossed these and other possibilities back and forth, on the night of October 4, the lights flickered as if mocking us, and then went out. For almost two hours, over 80 percent of Chile's population had no electricity. When it came back on, we managed to doze off fitfully. But, at 3:20 in the morning, a second blackout hit us. This one lasted till after the sun had risen.

Even the deepest of nights in any city accompanies you with some gleaming of pale and distant light, and it was the absence of even that dim radiance on my eyelids which alerted me and nudged me from my sleep. I did not know then, and still cannot prove now, who sabotaged Chile's electricity, but whoever it was

wanted the citizenry to go to bed in the dark and to rise in the dark. My nine-year-old son Joaquin may have been speaking for all of us. "Is he going to come and get me?" he asked. "Is that why he took off the lights?" Everybody in Chile knows who that "he" refers to. We would be punished, as we had been all these years, as if we were little children.

The terror was not only directed at the general's adversaries. We were afraid of what had been done to us: deportations, torture, jailings, raids, censorship, kidnappings, internal exile, mass executions, disappearances. But Pinochet's supporters were also frightened. The general had been telling them that hordes of terrorists and slumdwellers would descend upon them if the NO vote won. The fatherland was in danger of being thrown back into what the right wing calls the "mad chaos" of the Allende years. One of Pinochet's TV spots showed a steamroller crunching toys and furniture and inexorably advancing toward a beautiful little girl. For those planning to vote yes, the blackout was also interpreted as fearful and foreboding.

And yet, a few hours later, millions of Chileans were standing in line, determined to express their opinion for the first time in 15 years. By mid-morning, when I arrived at my polling station, a sprawling elementary school at the foot of the majestic Andes, thousands of men (women vote in corporate locales in Chile) were patiently awaiting their turn.

In the democratic times of Chile, election day had always been something to look forward to. Because you always cast your vote in the same place, you got to revisit on each occasion the same citizens that you had not seen in the interval, a small tribe reconvened for the purpose of celebrating our right to decide for ourselves who should govern us. This time, however, I was surrounded by faces I did not know. The coup had dispersed the people I had come to associate with balloting. My feelings were ambivalent. On the one hand, the men around me represented one more form of the devastation the military had visited upon our lives, how impossible it was to bring back the past. On the other hand, here we were again, in spite of Pinochet, determined to continue the interrupted historical tradition of our land—once the most democratic of Latin America. The dictatorship had tried to cut us off from each other, to deny us a space where we could meet and recognize our common existence—and now the ceremony among strangers had become one more step in a miraculous process of reconnection that had been developing during the last month.

The campaign had started on September 4 with an inspiring act by 300,000 people; but it had been more defiant than celebratory, with protesters unwilling to believe that we really could win. The last rally was on October 1 with well over a million people, relaxed, joyful, joking, anticipating victory. Behind the growth in numbers was the story of how so many opponents of Pinochet had broken their silence, stepped out of the shadow of their homes, and showed themselves publicly. We had finally gone beyond the large but constricted contingent of dissidents who had been risking their lives all these years. The majority of Chileans had finally found the courage to put their bodies where their hearts had always been. We had conquered fear, seclusion, and atomization.

A rush of feelings came over me as I entered the polling booth. My first reaction surprised me. I was indignant. I had never seen a replica of the vote itself—and I found it obscene that there should be only one name on the ballot, that of Augusto Pinochet Ugarte. A reminder that this was not an open, free election—that even if we beat the general, he could still, according to his own fraudulent Constitution of 1980, legally remain in office until March of 1990 and stay as well as commander-in-chief of the army for another five years. But I also felt alive—alive with those who could not vote, the executed, the disappeared, the exiles who had been let in too late to register, the exiles who had died abroad of sorrow or of cancer. We had to vote for them.

Trembling, I marked my vote NO.

At 7:30 in the evening—one hour later than promised, and three hours after the first *mesas* had closed—Alberto Cardemil, the undersecretary of the interior, released the first results which, to nobody's astonishment, showed the YES with 57.36 percent against 40.54 percent for the NO. What was worrisome was that the government had selected 79 *mesas* from around the country, representing a mere 0.36 percent of the vote—in order to give the impression that Pinochet was winning.

Cardemil transmitted his data from the Edificio Diego Portales, the tallest, most impressive building in Chile—constructed, by one of those ironies of history, by Salvador Allende in the early 1970s for the UNCTAD Conference, with the promise that it would later become the Palace of Culture of the Chilean People. Directly across from it, on the other side of the Alameda, Santiago's main avenue, in what foreign correspondents remarked to be an extremely appropriate David against Goliath symbol, was a desultory, two-story hall which housed the NO Command's press center. The NO leaders were not giving out information yet, because they wanted data that would be substantial and confirmed—at least 500,000 votes. A few blocks away, the PPD, one of the three opposition parties, had unofficial results showing the NO winning overwhelmingly. Why didn't they then announce this quickly, before another blackout? The PPD couldn't because they had accepted that only the No Command would speak that night. It was also dangerous to invite millions of Chileans to celebrate that early; provocateurs could turn this into an uncontrollable situation and give the regime the pretext to cancel the election.

Finally, a bit after nine o'clock, the NO Command hurriedly gave its first results—with just slightly more than 200,000 votes—a clear trend toward victory for the NO.

Wandering around Santiago, I found the people euphoric and dazed, eyes glazed by disbelief and faces wary.

A quick count by an independent committee shows the NO vote with over 55 percent nationally. Even in small rural towns where the military have ruled without a peep from the opposition, the NO vote is ahead. Rumors circulate that the black berets of the army are awaiting orders to take over the streets.

I decide to go home. If there is going to be trouble, I prefer to be with my family.

We live in a housing development of 16 modest bungalows where everybody knows everybody else and even the cats vote against Pinochet. The atmosphere among the neighbors was one of cautious, contained exhilaration—they were not going to let loose their feelings until someone in the government recognized our triumph.

That recognition came very slowly. Jarpa, a former Pinochet minister of the interior, and the head of Renovación Nacional, a right wing party that had supported Pinochet with reservations, admitted on television that the NO vote was clearly ahead. Moments later, the more hardline YES parties announced they were winning by 0.3 percent and had therefore decided to go off to bed—a less frank and elegant way of accepting defeat than Jarpa's. A friend called and told me that the Diego Portales was like a mausoleum. On the second floor, there was a banquet of lavish food that no one was eating and, naturally, hundreds of unopened champagne bottles.

Then Fernando Matthei, the head of the air force, stated on his way in to a meeting with Pinochet that the NO vote had clearly won.

All Chile had been waiting for that signal. Pandemonium broke loose. There were around 12 of us listening to the radio in a neighbor's house and we streamed out the door in total delirium to shout ourselves hoarse, hugging everybody in the vicinity, mingling with the echoes of other songs on the same street and the honking of thousands of horns and blowing of whistles all over the city.

It may seem bizarre that so many civilians, dedicated democrats, should have waited for the word from a military officer to celebrate. But we automatically understood that Matthei had preempted Pinochet's efforts to invalidate the election—the unanimity among the armed forces had crumbled. And in effect, two hours later, Cardemil told a weary world that, with a bit over 5 million votes counted, the NO had 53 percent to the 44 percent of the YES.

In the midst of the dancing and singing and hugging and boozing and tears and laughter that filled these hours, what I felt was relief and pride. Pinochet had taken my country captive for 15 years and not all the humiliations, not all the terror, not all the lies in the universe, had been able to rob us, ultimately, of our dignity. In the most despairing moments of these years, in the shadows of exile, as I watched so many people in Chile stand by helplessly while Pinochet had ravaged our soul, in the depths of that sadness, I had always kept up hope that a part of us had remained clean and pure and full of memory and full of the future.

The day that had started in darkness ended, in the middle of the night, in the defeat of a darkness which the people of Chile had never really made theirs.

The night of Thursday, October 6, however, at nine in the evening, as hundreds of thousands of people were spontaneously celebrating the victory, giving flowers to the police, calling for reconciliation with our opponents, shouting they had beaten Pinochet with a pencil, the lights blacked out again. Not a window was broken, not a person was hurt—though the streets were filled with throngs that could have gone wild. We showed the same order and discipline and adulthood we had shown during the electoral process, that had allowed us to survive the most ferocious dictatorship in contemporary Latin America.

Half an hour later, when the lights came on, there was Pinochet on TV, in full uniform, conceding defeat, but also stating he would stay on as president, he would not change the Constitution, he was the real victor.

Bands of right-wing hoodlums understood the message. They roamed the streets beating up and shooting the people of the NO vote. Soldiers fired from barracks. The minister of the interior insisted that Pinochet was the real winner.

In fact, I just heard Pinochet's wife say on the radio that the Constitution should be modified—to allow the general to be a candidate in next year's open elections.

The battle for the soul of Chile has just begun.

From: "Beyond the Blackout: How Chile Beat Pinochet with a Pencil," Village Voice, *October 18, 1988.*

EPILOGUE: OCTOBER 1989
ARIEL DORFMAN

The day after the plebiscite, the people of Santiago madly took over the streets and flocked to La Moneda, our presidential palace, shouting "Adios General"— goodbye forever to Pinochet.

In a sense, that wild celebration may have been premature. Not only has Pinochet been around in the year since the plebiscite, but he promises to remain among us for an even longer period, perhaps as commander-in-chief of the army for eight years after a democratic government is elected, perhaps as a shadowy presence perverting and thwarting every effort we make to liberate ourselves, certainly in our nightmares and the nightmares of our children's children. The unjust economic structure that has left almost half the population in abject poverty, the effect of prolonged and systematic terror on the citizenry, the authoritarian strains that tense each institution and experience, the lack of housing, educational facilities, health care—will haunt Chile for many long years to come. The military that he has brought permanently into the political arena will be watchful, ready to veto any changes in the status quo, the very changes that could attack the roots and causes of the dictatorship and therefore block the infinite replication of other Pinochets.

But in another sense, our insolent adieu to the general was irrefutably prophetic.

A dictator cannot reign unless he promises eternity. He must guarantee that, no matter what he or any of his cohorts does, he and they will never be held accountable. In that sense, every dictator attempts to abolish time, freeze history, colonize space with his image. The moment that people can sight his end and begin to conceive a world without him, his power begins to crumble. The erosion that Pinochet has suffered since the plebiscite can therefore be seen as foretelling his ultimate displacement from future power, a day when he is no more than a sad synonym in some dictionary of horror.

But the plebiscite itself was not won by a few million people who suddenly decided that they had suffered enough. It was won because during every minute of Pinochet's reign there were countless Chileans who dared to dream that history had not been frozen and that they could make a difference and who turned that defiance into a series of small laborious steps that, inch by inch, took the country away from the dictator, set apart zones that he could not command. Historians will point to the creation of thousands of associations, trade unions, alternative communication networks, soup kitchens, human rights organizations, student unions, cultural centers, church groups, and—yes—photographers who were not willing to let the image of hope and horror disappear. But none of this could have been possible if previously, simultaneously, there had not flared in multiple hearts a blaze of resistance, a fierce collective decision not to accept that tyranny should have the final word.

In the years to come, it will be up to those men and women to prove that, when all was said, when all was done, when all was captured in the right images, the general was, after all, not eternal.

Shortly before curfew, Santiago

5   As the Hawker Hunter airplanes with their charge of bombs for La Moneda buzzed through the sky over downtown Santiago, one by one, each radio station took up the nationwide broadcast of marching music interrupted from time to time by the latest martial decrees. Some did so happily complying with the new authorities. Other stations went on reporting up to the instant the soldiers forced their way into the studio, when their programming also fell into step.

That evening, the curfew began about 6 P.M. and lasted some 42 hours. And from then on, under various states of exception (state of siege, state of emergency etc.), restrictions on evening or night circulation continued for well over 10 years. The curfew became so much a part of Chilean life, being snipped back over such a long time, varying from town to town, eventually from weekday to weekend, season to season, that nobody seems to remember exactly when they were again granted the right to move freely about the streets at any hour of day or night.

Chonchi, island of Chiloe

7   "I'm always thinking they're coming to get me again. When I see a strange car in the neighborhood, I'm up at the window, trying to see what it's doing. I write down the license number. I have a notebook full of license numbers, as many as ten a day." From: Patricia

Politizer's interview with "Pedro" in her book, *La Ira de Pedro y los Otros* (Editorial Planeta, Espejo de Chile, 1988)

19

In the mid-1970s, mothers who couldn't afford to feed their children at home collectively organized neighborhood lunch programs known as children's dining rooms. By pooling their own resources and working together, they became eligible for monthly quotas of milk, oil, flour, and dried goods that Catholic and other relief agencies offered.

These initial self-help organizations formed to combat hunger, the poor's most urgent problem. They also acted as stepping stones to the growth of various groups within the communities. In an effort to raise money for the dining rooms as well as supplement their families' meager incomes, women baked and sold bread, formed handicraft and trade workshops, created sewing and knitting circles, marketing their handicraft products. Others formed health committees, first to learn and later to teach their neighbors about first aid, hygiene, nutrition, and how to treat the most endemic ailments in their communities.

Communal meal,
Villa Francia, Santiago

21

On a dry autumn day in April, more than 100 delegates from the Mapuche reservations of Malalhue, Chelle, Changue, Quechecahuin, Peleco, Nueva Malley, Comoe, Boyeco, and others met in Puerto Dominguez to review the range of the New Law for Indian Affairs decreed by General Pinochet on March 22, 1979. The new law set out mechanisms that threatened the communal ownership of the reservations'

Mapuche Indians,
Puerto Dominguez

land virtually at the whim of any one occupant. It could be executed at the "written request of any occupant of such lands," and "following its inscription in the Public Deeds Office the estates resulting from the division of the reserves will cease to be considered Indian lands and their grantees Indians." The main concern for the 43,000 families still living on reservations in the 8th, 9th and 10th regions is that their lands could end up eventually in the hands of the *huinca*, or non-Mapuche.

Inside the Vicaria, Santiago

26   The Vicaria de la Solidaridad was created on January 1, 1978, by Cardenal Raul Silva Henriquez, Archbishop of Santiago, to continue work in the defense and promotion of human rights previously carried out by an ecumenical organization, the Pro Peace Committee. It was created following General Pinochet's order to dissolve the Pro Peace Committee, when the visible heads of that organization were sent into exile.

One of the principal services of the Vicaria has been to provide legal defense for citizens hard put to find a lawyer elsewhere: the persecuted. Defending dissidents of the military regime and their families, often victims of the excesses committed by members of the armed forces or of extremist death squads, the Vicaria has been awarded numerous prizes for its work: 1978—United Nations Human Rights Award; 1980—Vladimir Herzog Journalism Award (Brazil); 1984—Bruno Kreisky Foundation Award (Austria); 1984—Prince of Asturias Liberty Award (Spain); 1986—Letelier-Moffit Award for Human Rights (USA); 1987—Carter-Manil Foundation Award (USA); 1988—Simon Bolivar Award, UNESCO.

Classes began late in 1985. A March 5th earthquake that shook Santiago's foundations harder than any in the last 100 years had delayed them. Jose Manuel Parada's children were still having a hard time getting to school before the bell at 8:30 A.M. He was dropping them off on his way to work in the Vicaria de la Solidaridad, where he was director of the Archive and Processing Unit. He was in a hurry when he stopped to talk to Manuel Guerrero, president of the Teacher's Union and professor at the Colegio Latino Americano de Integración, a private school in the Providencia area. As they spoke, a police helicopter flew over the school close enough to shake the building, stirring memories of the quake in the children's minds. A block away, someone diverted the heavy morning traffic away from the busy street that ran in front of the school.

At 8:40, a beige Chevrolet stationwagon approached the pair talking on the sidewalk. Three gunmen stepped out and grabbed Parada and Guerrero. Leopoldo Munoz, a teacher at the school, tried to intervene, but a heavy blow from a pistol butt stopped him. He heard the command "Shoot him" and felt the bullet hit his stomach. The kidnapper's car sped away.

Forty-eight hours later, the bodies of Parada and Guerrero were found in the bushes near Quilicura next to a road to the airport. With them was the body of Santiago Nattino. The throats of all three had been slit.

The investigation of Judge Jose Canovas culminated in the indictment of members of the DICOMCAR, a unit within the police. The following day, on August 2, 1986, General Cesar Mendoza, director of the national police force, Carabineros, and member of the governing junta since the 1973 coup, resigned.

Wake for Jose Manuel Parada, human rights worker kidnapped and assassinated

Vigil for the detained
and disappeared

30   The majority of the cases involving the disappearance of political prisoners were produced during the years immediately following the military takeover (1973–1977).

In a presentation to the Supreme Court made November 3, 1976, the Episcopal Vicars of the Cardenal Archbishop of Santiago suggested a long list of interrogations possible if any investigation concerning the joint destiny of hundreds of missing prisoners was opened. Although individual cases had been brought to the courts previously, none had been solved. Now the priests were pointing to the idea of wide-ranging investigation of all the cases in conjunction, and pointing to possible clues. The list named 24 members of the armed forces and 6 members of the secret police known as the DINA, as well as the commanding officers in charge of the prison camps in Tejas Verdes and Cuatro Alamos as people the courts could question.

They also asked that the persons in charge of the DINA torture centers in the Villa Grimaldi, and in Jose D. Canas, Iran, and Londres streets in Santiago, and the DINA clinic in Santa Lucia, the Parachuters' School in Peldehue, the basement of the Ministry Serena and Santiago, the School of Army Sub-Officers, the Osorno Regiment, the Engineering Regiment in Copiapo, the air force base in Colina, the Silva Palma Barrack, the military hospital, the school in Linares, and two police stations in Santiago and one in Lonquimay. They also recommended finding the owners of 13 cars, 8 of which were Chevrolet C-10 vans preferred by the "security forces," giving the license plate numbers.

The information for a possible investigation was based on testimony of the last sighting of the missing persons, often given by fellow prisoners, by witnesses of their kidnappings, or by families who had managed to follow the shifting location of their arrested relatives until a final dead end.

When Army General Manuel Contreras, commanding officer of the secret police known as the DINA, was implicated in the 1976 car bomb assassination of Orlando Letelier on the streets of Washington, D.C., the disappearances dwindled. By 1978, when the DINA was dissolved, to be replaced by the CNI, with a handful of exceptions (one in 1984, five in 1987), the disappearances ended.

In an attempt to solve their dire housing problems, **31** some 250 families tried to occupy low-cost government-subsidized houses in the municipality of Puente Alto, in mid-May 1984, and were violently expelled by police. The housing was destined for people from various other municipalities whose homemade shanty-towns were being knocked down and who were being relocated.

Land takeover, Puente Alto

In Puente Alto, the 4,000 families of *"allegados"* composes only a small portion of the estimated 135,000 families who live as "extras" in the shantytowns all over Santiago. Not exactly homeless, they are generally young couples (between 18 and 30) with small children who have no alternative but to move in with relatives or whoever will take them in, sometimes getting special permission from the mayor to put up their one-room shack in a stranger's yard. Most have no economic capacity for accumulating savings that could give them the right to apply for government housing subsidies.

Weekly vigil by the families of
the victims of repression
in front of La Moneda

32 Families of the detained disappeared, accompanied by the widows of three professionals murdered in 1985, stage a weekly demonstration outside the presidential palace in their ongoing search for justice. The number of the detained disappeared in Chile is much lower than those missing in Argentina. Many attribute this fact to the public and judicial denunciations made by a handful of brave women who were not afraid to exhaust all possibilities in their investigation of the destiny of their children, spouses, and siblings.

Carmen Gloria Quintana
with the Sebastian Acevedo
Anti-Torture Movement

34 On July 2, 1988, at approximately 8 A.M., Carmen Gloria Quintana and Rodrigo Rojas were taken into custody by an army patrol under the command of Lieutenant Pedro Fernandez Dittus. When another patrol arrived with tires, gasoline, and a molotov cocktail found a block and a half away, the fury of the captors increased. After a beating that lasted 10 minutes, Quintana and Rojas were sprayed with gasoline and set afire (in circumstances yet unclarified by the Chilean courts). They were then gathered up in blankets and thrown in the back of the army truck. Their charred, semi-conscious bodies were found in a dry ditch in Quilicura, not far from where labor leader Tucapel Jimenez was found with his throat slit in 1982 and Jose Manuel Parada, Manuel Guerrero, and Santiago Nattino, also with slit throats, in 1985. Carmen Gloria urged Rodrigo into consciousness, forced him to get up and walk. They found their way to a country road, where they were picked up and driven to the emergency hospital. Rodrigo died as a result of his burns four days later. Carmen Gloria was sent to Canada for special treatment and rehabilitation. Lieutenant Fernandez was promoted to captain while awaiting trial in the military courts.

In the first days of November 1983, some 24 people were arrested by personnel of the National Center of Information, known as the CNI. They were being held in a secret place of detention. Sebastian Acevedo, a factory worker whose children were among the arrested, presented a writ of habeus corpus in favor of his two children, Maria and Galo, but received no reply from the courts. He wrote a letter to the Intendente Brigadier General Eduardo Ibanez, but there was no answer. Some of the 24 who had been released told of the torture they had suffered. Doctors confirmed their testimony after examinations. Acevedo's children were still being held.

On November 11th, he made a drastic decision. Armed with a can of gasoline and matches, Sebastian Acevedo went to the central plaza of the southern city Concepcion. He doused his body with the flammable liquid and set himself afire.

Not long before Acevedo's death, a group of clergy, seminary students, and lay Catholics began a series of demonstrations calling for the end of torture. Using tactics of active nonviolence, they began sit-ins in front of torture centers and headquarters of the secret police, on the steps of the Supreme Court, in front of media offices whose news reports omitted the topic, pointing accusing fingers at the perpetrators, voicing in unison the names of the victims. Following his dramatic suicide, they became the Sebastian Acevedo Anti-Torture Movement.

35

Demonstration in front of the National Library

Searching for Colonel Carreno,
Santiago

36   On September 1, 1987, Army Colonel Carlos Carreno was kidnapped by the guerrilla group the Frente Patriotico Manuel Rodriguez. During the three months the colonel was held by his captors, the armed forces carried on a virtual house-to-house search. Although search and seize operations were not uncommon in the poorer neighborhoods, this was the first time that wealthier residential areas were affected.

The kidnappers asked for a ransom to be distributed in foodstuffs among the poor in specific communities in Santiago. Following this, Carreno was freed on December 2nd near the offices of the morning paper *O Estado de São Paulo* in the Brazilian city of São Paulo 92 days after his kidnapping.

Student wounded during a sit-in
at the University of Chile

37   "The scarce opposition press never realized how it collaborated with the government. The accounts of torture, the reports about the unscrupulous actions of the political police, were chilling.

"The young were cautioned: 'Don't speak out! Forget your name! Don't even think of your ideals! Be patient, endure!' Theater plays that accused, economically strangled by a special tax and limited audiences, insisted on showing what happened to the ones who dared resist. Their message was obvious, but unseen: this will happen to you if you speak the truth, if you think, if you oppose what is happening. The public grew angry, felt part of a common cause, left furious. But when they returned home, they repeated to their children, 'Be careful. Don't speak above a whisper. Be deaf, blind, dumb.' Learn the subtle traitors' vocation of survival. We became experts. And guilty." Marco Antonio de la Parra

The halls and balconies of the Chilean Human Rights Committee were packed with journalists, cameramen, and foreign diplomats, including U.S. ambassador to Santiago Harry Barnes. Across the street the doors of the Basilica del Salvador Church had been closed since the 1985 earthquake had brought the roof down behind the altar. Rodrigo Roja's funeral was being held outside to accommodate the throngs now filling the streets so densely that it was suffocating in spite of the warm, sunny weather. When the police vehicles began to arrive, the crowd grew apprehensive. Between the commemorative speeches someone at the microphone announced that the nearest commissioner had assured them that the police had no objection to the funeral taking place on the steps outside the church.

Huge police water cannon trucks arrived at the far end of the street. Smaller wagons known as skunks, for their habit of spraying crowds with mace or other types of high-power tear or nausea-producing gases appeared on side streets. Those on the edge of the crowd held up the palm of their hands in a gesture to show themselves unarmed and untainted by others' blood. From the center accusing fingers were pointed at the uniformed personnel.

Within seconds, the bobbing heads of the crowd running for cover were barely visible under the dense smoke of tear gas. As it rose to the second-story balconies of the Commission, the gas was blinding the cameramen, Ambassador Barnes was being ushered down a hallway, handkerchief to face, trying to escape the penetrating cloud. Miraculously, the charge of the water cannons through the brimming street below, whirling its high-power blast through scattering backs, left no trail of run-over bodies.

Funeral for Rodrigo Rojas

"Skunks" followed them, driving with two tires upon the narrow sidewalks to get a closer shot of people who had pressed their bodies against the sides of buildings in their urge to avoid the blast of water and gas or tread of wheels.

In the middle of this mayhem, the hearse began what attempted to be a slow, steady pace toward the cemetery. The crowd refused to be dispersed. They scattered only to avoid immediate danger and then to regroup in their procession. A few blocks further on, a group joined hands around the hearse. There were shots, probably tear gas guns, and firm hands guided choking mourners into nearby apartment buildings. Voices cried out, "Breathe close to the ground, it isn't as thick!" "Don't rub your eyes, that only makes it worse!" "Have a bite of my lemon," "Put some salt on the back of your tongue," "Take a sniff of ammonia, it'll clear you up!" Outside the police were clubbing people, but through the storm of gas and falling water, it was difficult to see if anyone was being arrested. Out of the tempest, the hearse emerged surrounded not by mourners, save one man on the hood of the car defensively raising his hand, but by tall, helmeted policemen wielding nightsticks and a motorcycle squad that quickly rushed away.

The group outside the church doubled and tripled their numbers during the two-hour wait at the grave before the arrival of the burnt remains of Rodrigo Rojas. U.S. State Department spokesperson Bernard Kalb said of the funeral, "The breaking up of what would have been a solemn ceremony was clearly the responsibility of the Chilean security forces."

On the evening of September 4, 1984, Father Andre Jarlan, a French missionary priest, went upstairs just before dark to read his Bible in the bedroom of the house he shared with Father Pierre Dubois. It was a simple brick and wood construction, like other homes in the *poblacion* La Victoria where he lived and worked. A national protest had been called for this day, and it had been long and exhausting. It began in the morning with the death of a 25-year-old youth, and several others had been wounded during its course. A boy close to Andre had been severely maltreated. The priest was saddened and shocked.

Outside the atmosphere was calm around the flaming barricades. Made of burning tires, they were an attempt to delay the entry of government security forces. Just after 6 P.M. the police arrived, opening fire in the streets below his window, where demonstrators protesting the long years of Pinochet regime scattered to take cover. Two bullets pierced the thin wooden walls of the second story. When Father Pierre arrived at 7:20, he found Andre slumped over the desk, his hand on the open Bible, apparently sleeping, with a bullethole in his neck.

On September 11, 1986, Father Pierre Dubois, also a French missionary priest, was expelled from Chile. Other foreign priests expelled by the government included: Father Guido Peters (Belgian), 1987; Father Jaime Lancelot (French), and Father Daniel Carruette (French), 1986; Father Dennis O'Mara (American), 1984; Father Desmond McGillicuddy (Irish), Father Brendan Forde (Irish), and Father Brian Mahon (Irish), 1983.

42

Funeral for Father Andre Jarlan

18,000 army troops patrol
the streets of Santiago

When the leader of the Copper Workers Confederation (CTC), Adolfo Seguel, first called for a nationwide day of protest to be held on May 11, 1983, "to express through active nonviolence the profound distress of both workers and citizens for the unjust, miserable situation to which we are being subjected by an economically, socially, and politically oppressive regime that leaves us out in the cold," even he was overwhelmed by the massive participation of all sectors of the nation. Attendance dropped 50 percent in public schools and 70 percent in private; university students held assemblies and other actions on 10 campuses; 200 lawyers conducted a sit-in in the Supreme Court, followed by a silent march through the center, where they were applauded by bystanders. Some blue and white collar unions went on strike for the day, while others held a slowdown, arriving late on the job and refusing to eat in company cafeterias, banging their spoons on the tables. Bank clerks had a symbolic five-minute strike. Consumers boycotted stores and diminished public transportation.

At 8 P.M. the pot banging began from the poor neighborhoods to the upper-class areas. Timidly at first, it crescendoed as people realized that their neighbors were also voicing their discontent. Barricades went up like great bonfires surrounded by percussion orchestras as people rejoiced in a carnival that clearly said to one and all, "We are not alone!" Honking car caravans filled the main street of upper-class Providencia.

The party was not, however, without a cost. Two died from bullet wounds fired from unmarked cars, and 350 were arrested. But the opposition scored the protest as a grand success, and they were to continue for one day each month for the rest of the year. In the days that followed that first protest, on August 11, 1983, only one month before the tenth anniversary of the military coup that put Pinochet in power, 18,000 troops were sent to patrol the streets of Santiago. The following morning the newspapers spoke of over 50 deaths, while government figures put the body count at 17, with 60 showing bullet wounds. On any dusty street of the poor neighborhoods, children held up the empty shells of shot guns and automatic rifles that testified to their night of terror.

The "Don't forget me" campaign of various women's groups began shortly before the 1988 plebiscite, when the women feared that all the talk of a national reconciliation, the key message of Pope John Paul II's visit to Chile in August 1987, could be interpreted as an invitation to forgive and forget all the human rights abuses committed during the years of the military regime.

The lifesize silhouettes bearing the names of victims of violence, the question "Have you forgotten me?" and a simiIation of the yes/no option of the upcoming plebescite were first carried through the streets of downtown Santiago on August 29, 1988, the day before Augusto Pinochet was nominated as the one and only candidate in the event. Rising above a wave of over 1,000 silent, marching women and surrounded by the applause of bystanders, they invaded the center. By the time the police arrived, most of the women had merged back into the crowd, leaving their symbolic companion to line the streets, occupy the city benches. Few of the women were arrested, but the accusing styrofoam images were stomped on, thrown

49

"Have you forgotten me?"
Figures representing the
victims of repression, Santiago

askew by water cannons and "arrested," to be taken away in police vans. One of the women who went to the nearest police station early to see which women would be taken off the vans following the demonstration said she saw the police stop next to an empty, high-walled lot to throw the broken silhouettes over the fence. "They treated them just like the people they were meant to represent," she said.

"No more because there are more of us," International Women's Day, Santiago

50   "The politics of spectacle requires personal preparation, and the Mujeres por la Vida (Women for Life) set about training women. Before the march in rich neighborhoods, they helped women get ready for the increasing danger. The women were asked to figure out their own level of fear and then expose themselves to the things that scare them before the demonstration. If they were afraid of facing the police, they were told simply to find a policeman and stare at him until they could see him as a man and not as a representative of the state. The women were told to circle police vans on foot, until the hated symbols of the regime appeared just as another kind of motor vehicle. The women were to talk about their terrors among themselves and find others, with the same level of fear, with whom they could march in affinity groups.

The women also instructed one another about how to deal with the tear gas. Women for Life instructed participants to stop eating two hours before demonstrations, to dress in casual clothing, to take off eye makeup but to put cream and salt on their cheekbones to keep tear gas powder from entering their eyes. The women learned to carry lemons to avoid tear gas sting and to bring a jar with homemade smelling salts made of salt dampened with ammonia.

"Thus prepared, International Women's Day, Friday, March 7, 1986, women from throughout Santiago met in a downtown park. When the police drove them out, they disrupted traffic by dancing in groups down the major arteries of the downtown area." From: Valdes, Temma Kaplan, and Majorie Agosin, "The Politics of Spectacle in Chile" The Barnard Occasional Papers on Women's Issues, Fall 1987.

General Pinochet wore the tricolor presidential band during a ceremony commemorating the anniversary of the 1980 Constitution. According to the Washington-based International Human Rights Law Group, in their book *Chile: The Plebiscite and Beyond*:

"The 1980 Constitution is designed to perpetuate the 'protected democracy.' Under this constitution, General Pinochet holds virtual control of the national and local government. He personally has the authority to appoint the commanders-in-chief of the army.

"The 1980 Constitution legalized extraordinary restrictions on human rights and civil liberties. Under various states of exception, the government may imprison persons without charge and hold them incommunicado for up to 20 days, restrict the right of assembly and freedom of information and opinion, impose censorship on mail and communications, expel persons from Chile, or order them into internal exile for up to three months. . . .

"Law 18.662 provides that all organizations, movements, and parties declared unconstitutional (under Article 8) lose their civil and legal status, including any right to express opinions publicly. It imposes penalties on anyone who acts as an apologist for or 'accepts the support' of any such entities or its representatives during any electoral exercise."

53

General Augusto Pinochet Ugarte
at Diego Portales, Santiago

BIOGRAPHIES OF THE CONTRIBUTORS

MARCO ANTONIO DE LA PARRA

Born Santiago, 1952. A practicing psychiatrist by profession, but best known as a playwright and received the 1987 Chilean Critics' Award for his work in this area. His plays have been brought to the stage in ten European, North and South American countries. Three plays (*Secret Obscenities*; *Beds*; *Every Young Woman's Desire*) have been translated into English. His first novel *Holy War* was published in Santiago, 1989.

ARIEL DORFMAN

Born Argentina. A Chilean citizen forced into exile in 1973. Author of *How To Read Donald Duck* and *The Empire's Old Clothes*, both nonfiction; the novels *Mascara*, *The Last Song of Manuel Sendero*, and *Widows*; *Last Waltz in Santiago and Other Poems of Exile and Disappearance*; and the plays *Widows* and *Reader*. His books have been translated into twenty languages.

A professor at Duke University, Dorfman is a regular contributor to *The New York Times*, the *Los Angeles Times*, *The Nation*, and *The Village Voice*.

PAZ ERRAZURIZ

Born Santiago, 1944. Elementary school teacher before coming to photography in early 1970s. Portraiture both in her commercial and personal work reflects her interest in people on the periphery of society, the marginal sectors, the minorities. Founding member of the Association of Independent Photographers (AFI). Awarded a Guggenheim grant, 1986. Free-lances for various publications.

ALEJANDRO HOPPE

Born Santiago, 1961. Has covered principal political events of the last few years, first as a free-lance, then since 1987 as staff photographer for *La Epoca* newspaper. Founder of photo collective FOCO, member of AFI and Union of Graphic Reporters (URG).

ALVARO HOPPE

Born Santiago, 1956. Former actor, took up photography in 1983. Staff photographer for opposition weekly *Apsi* for five years, now free-lances for national and foreign press. Member of AFI, FOCO, and URG.

HELEN HUGHES

Born Oklahoma, USA, 1948. Grew up in Europe (1963–1970). Has lived in Chile since 1971, when she began working in photography. Started in journalism as staff photographer for the Vicaria's biweekly *Solidaridad* (1977–1982). Free-lancing for national and foreign press since then. Founding member AFI.

JORGE IANISZEWSKI

Born Santiago, 1949. Studied cinema and worked editing and directing documentaries and newsreels (1971–1973) for Chile Films. Free-lancing in photography since 1974, principally for Chilean and foreign magazines. The founding president of AFI in 1981, and in 1985 helped form the local photo agency Fotobanco. During the 1980s created a number of slide shows for social organizations and promotional work.

HECTOR LOPEZ

Born Santiago, 1955. Initially doing weddings, ID pictures, and publicity photos to pay for his studies in design and photography, he began to free-lance for local press in 1982. In 1984, he went on to teach photography in different educational institutes, including a photo workshop in the *poblacion* La Victoria that lasted two and one-half years. Head of the photography department of the Escuela Superior de Estudios since 1986. Present president of AFI, FOCO, and URG.

KENA LORENZINI

Born Talca (southern Chile), 1959. Began working as a staff photographer for opposition magazines in early 1980s, the first years with *Hoy* and, following a year of work in Europe, with *Analisis*. Continues to free-lance for various publications and institutions. Member AFI.

JUAN DOMINGO MARINELLO

Born Iquique (northern Chile), 1948. Studied art and journalism in the Catholic University (UC) (1966–1970), and in Germany 1974–1975. Graphic reporter for AMEUROPRESS, European and local publications. Founding member AFI. Teaches photography in UC, journalism school, head of photography in the Santiago studio/lab/agency Taller Uno.

SUSAN MEISELAS

Born Maryland, USA. A free-lance photographer and member of Magnum Photos. She is the author of *Carnival Strippers* and *Nicaragua* and a contributor and co-editor of *El Salvador: Work of 30 Photographers.*

CHRISTIAN MONTECINO

Born Santiago, 1946. Grew up between Santiago and Washington, D.C., where he worked as a photographer for the International Monetary Fund. He moved back to Chile with his wife and two children in July 1973, to begin free-lancing. On October 16, 1973, army personnel removed him from his residence during curfew at 6 A.M. The same morning, the new military authorities would be taking up offices in the building across the street from his apartment. It was only through family connections that his body was recovered from the morgue. He had been summarily shot along with the others arrested the same morning from the same apartment building.

MARCELO MONTECINO

Born Santiago, 1943. Grew up in Washington, D.C., where he studied political science and Latin American literature at George Washington University. Has been photographing all his life, combines interpreting with documentary photography for worldwide press as well as fact-finding tours for international organizations. Based in Washington until 1987, when he moved back to Chile, has been covering Central and South America since the late 1960s. Member AFI. In 1980, an international jury headed by Gabriel Garcia Marquez and Julio Cortázar awarded him first prize in a contest that led to the publication of his book *Con Sangre en el Ojo* in Mexico, 1981.

OSCAR NAVARRO

Born Santiago, 1960. Began photographing at the age of 13 in the studio of his father, a professional photographer, stage set designer, and director of photography for cinema, who also taught in the film school of the Catholic University. Began free-lancing for local and foreign press 1983. Staff photographer in opposition daily *El Fortin Mapocho* 1987–1988. Awarded title "International Grand Master" by the International Press Organization, 1987. Member AFI.

CLAUDIO PEREZ

Born Santiago, 1957. Studied publicity design. In 1979 left for Brazil, where he did everything from leather work to publicity. Started photography at this time and, upon his return to Chile in 1983, began free-lancing for the São Paolo photo agency F4. In 1986, he, PAULO SLACHEVSHY, and OSCAR NAVARRO participated in the book *El Pan Nuestro de Cada Dia*, edited in Chile and requisitioned by the authorities prior to distribution. Awarded bronze medal in the photo essay and news photo category of the 1987 International Press Organization contest. Member AFI, FOCO.

SERGIO PEREZ

Born Santiago, 1962. Studied design and architecture in the Catholic University of Valparaiso, Chile, 1979–1984. Has worked as a free-lance photographer and layout designer since then, particularly for the educational magazine *¿Que Hacemos?* and the quarterly publication of cultural critique *Kappa*.

LUIS POIROT

Born Santiago, 1940. Photographer since 1964. Resided in Paris (1973–1974) and Barcelona (1975–1986), where he worked for the Spanish paper *El Pais* and various publishing houses. Author of book *Neruda: Absence and Presence* (Chile, 1986; Spain, 1987; USA, 1990). Teaches photography in the Catholic University. Has also directed a number of plays for theater produced in Chile and abroad.

PAULO SLACHEVSKY

Born Santiago, 1964. Lived in France from 1975 to 1983, when he returned to Chile. Started taking photographs during the first national protests, 1983. Free-lancing for Chilean and foreign media since then. Won bronze medal in the photo essay category of the International Press Organization contest in 1987. Member AFI.

LUIS WEINSTEIN

Born in Santiago, 1957. Began free-lancing in 1980 in publicity and editorial photography. Teaches photography in Foto Forum, a private school of which he is part owner. His work is included in various European collections. Member AFI.

OSCAR WITTKE

Born Santiago, 1957. His studies ranged from medicine and architecture to aesthetics and journalism in the Catholic University, 1977–1982. Started photography in 1979 with a number of slide presentations called "Valparaiso." Received the "Amigos del Arte" corporation grant to carry on personal work in photos in 1986. Free-lance photographer since 1984, he has also published poetry in various local cultural reviews and completed two novels he hopes to publish in the future as a trilogy. Member AFI.

1 LUIS POIROT, 1970
2 LUIS POIROT, 1973
3 LUIS POIROT, 1973
4 HECTOR LOPEZ, 1986
5 HELEN HUGHES, 1981
6 PAZ ERRAZURIZ, 1987
7 MARCELO MONTECINO, 1980
8 OSCAR WITTKE, 1982
9 HELEN HUGHES, 1979
10 HECTOR LOPEZ, 1986
11 OSCAR WITTKE, 1983
12 PAZ ERRAZURIZ, 1985
13 PAZ ERRAZURIZ, 1981
14 PAZ ERRAZURIZ, 1988
15 LUIS WEINSTEIN, 1984
16 PAZ ERRAZURIZ, 1986
17 OSCAR WITTKE, 1987
18 CLAUDIO PEREZ, 1987
19 HELEN HUGHES, 1977
20 HELEN HUGHES, 1983
21 HELEN HUGHES, 1979
22 OSCAR WITTKE, 1986
23 JUAN DOMINGO MARINELLO, 1973
24 JUAN DOMINGO MARINELLO, 1973
25 MARCELO MONTECINO, 1988